Taxcafe Tax Guides

Tax-Free Property Investments

How to Earn 140% More Income and Retire Rich
with a Property Pension

By Nick Braun PhD

Important Legal Notices:

Taxcafe®
Tax Guide - "Tax-Free Property Investments"

Published by:
Taxcafe UK Limited
67 Milton Road
Kirkcaldy KY1 1TL
Tel: (0044) 01592 560081
Email: team@taxcafe.co.uk

Third edition, July 2009

ISBN 978-1-904608-98-1

About the Author & Taxcafe

Nick Braun founded Taxcafe in Edinburgh in 1999 along with his partner, Aileen Smith. As the driving force behind the company, their aim is to provide affordable plain-English tax information for private individuals and investors, business owners, IFAs and accountants.

In the last 10 years Taxcafe has become one of the best-known tax publishers in the UK and won several business awards.

Nick has been involved in the tax publishing world since 1989 as a writer, editor and publisher. He holds a masters degree and doctorate in economics from the University of Glasgow, where he was awarded the prestigious William Glen Scholarship and later became a Research Fellow. Prior to that he graduated with distinction from the University of South Africa, the country's oldest university, earning the highest results in economics in the university's history.

He went on to become editor of *Personal Finance* and *Tax Breaks*, two of South Africa's best-known financial publications before moving to the UK.

Nick and Aileen are very keen property investors and own a portfolio of buy-to-let flats in the Fife seaside town of Kirkcaldy, where the Taxcafe head office is based.

When he's not working, Nick likes to take his children to the zoo, relax with friends and eat good food.

Dedication

Once again, to Aileen for all your love and support and to Jake, Sandy and Tilly for all the joy you bring.

Thanks

Thank you to my parents, Ann and Deryck, for all your encouragement over the years. I would also like to thank my in-laws, Douglas and June, for the tremendous help and support you have given us.

Contents

Introduction   1

PART 1.   **PROPERTY ISAs**   5

Chapter 1. Introduction to Property ISAs   7

Chapter 2. Brand New Property Tax Shelters   11

Chapter 3. How to Earn 80% More from   18
Your Property Investments

PART 2.   **PROPERTY FUNDS**   25

Chapter 4.   Property Funds: The Benefits   27

Chapter 5.   Property Funds: The Drawbacks   43

Chapter 6.   Real Estate Investment Trusts: Answers to   51
All Your Questions

Chapter 7.   Directory of Real Estate Investment Trusts   56

Chapter 8.   Property Unit Trusts: Benefits & Drawbacks   61

Chapter 9.   Directory of Property Unit Trusts   65

Chapter 10. Property Investment Companies: 69
Benefits & Drawbacks

Chapter 11. Directory of Property Investment Companies   71

Chapter 12. Tax-free Overseas Property Investments   73

Contents (cont...)

PART 3. RETIRE RICH WITH A PROPERTY PENSION 85

Chapter 13. The Amazing Pension Tax Reliefs 87

Chapter 14. Plain-English Guide to the A-Day Pension Rules 111

Chapter 15. What Kind of Property Can You Put in a SIPP? 125

Chapter 16. How to Set Up and Run Your Own Property SIPP 139

PART 4. BRICKS & MORTAR vs PENSIONS & ISAs 147

Chapter 17. ISAs vs Bricks and Mortar: Detailed Example 149

Chapter 18. ISAs vs Pensions: Detailed Example 157

Chapter 19. Pensions vs Bricks and Mortar 166

Chapter 20. Pensions vs Bricks and Mortar: 171
Detailed Example

PART 5. MORE TAX-SAVING IDEAS 175

Chapter 21. ISAs vs Paying Off Your Mortgage 177

Chapter 22. The Best Self-select ISAs and ISA Supermarkets 182

Chapter 23. How to Save £3,636 Extra in Tax Every Year 185

Other Useful Taxcafe Products and Services 188

Disclaimer 194

Introduction

This book is all about making tax-free property investments in ISAs and self-invested personal pensions (SIPPs). It also contains a wealth of information about property funds such as real estate investment trusts (REITs), property unit trusts and property 'vulture funds', whose purpose is to snap up undervalued properties when the market is weak.

In recent years there have been some extremely important developments both in the property world and the tax-free investment world:

- In January 2006 ISA investors were allowed to invest tax-free in property unit trusts for the first time.

- In April 2006 the 'A-Day' pension changes came into operation, providing increased tax relief and flexibility for pension investors.

- In 2005 Gordon Brown performed one of his infamous u-turns, banning residential property from SIPPs. But in July 2006 the Finance Act revealed that certain types of residential property would still be allowed.

- In January 2007 the UK's first tax-free real estate investment trusts (REITs) were launched.

- In 2007 the UK commercial property market started to collapse. Some parts of the market have fallen by more than 50% and shares in many real estate investment trusts and other property funds have fallen by over 80%.

- In the middle of 2007 residential property finally gave up the ghost. Between August 2007 and June 2009 the Halifax House Price Index registered a 21% fall.

- Throughout 2008 almost every property unit trust started levying hefty exit penalties or placing a freeze on investor withdrawals to avoid being forced to sell properties on the cheap to raise cash. Despite these desperate actions their unit prices plummeted. Investors in Aviva Investors

Property Trust, the biggest and best-known fund, have seen 45% of the value of their investment wiped out.

- In the April 2009 Budget there was some good news. The annual ISA investment limit was increased from £7,200 to £10,200 (£5,100 for cash ISAs). The increases apply from 6th October 2009 for those aged 50+ and next year for everyone else.

- There was also some bad news in the Budget for high earners. From 6th April 2011 those earning £150,000 or more will have their pension tax relief reduced.

- While most of the big property fund managers have failed miserably to protect investors from the collapse in the property market, more entrepreneurial property experts have started setting up 'vulture funds' to purchase bargain properties. Many of these funds are open to the public and can be invested in tax free.

This guide examines all of these changes and explains how you can use them to make profitable tax-free property investments.

We kick off in Part 1 with property ISAs, one of the simplest and most tax-efficient ways to invest in property. First of all I'll explain why ISAs are such amazing tax shelters before looking at what types of property you can shelter inside them. We'll then move on to a fascinating example that shows how an ISA investor can earn 80% more money than someone who wastes this valuable tax break.

Part 2 is all about property funds. These powerful investments not only help you save tax, they also reduce many of the risks and problems faced by buy-to-let investors.

We start off with a detailed look at all the pros and cons of property funds before taking a closer look at the three types of fund available to both ISA and SIPP investors. These include real estate investment trusts, property unit trusts and property investment companies.

Part 3 looks at the fascinating world of property SIPPs. We kick off with a detailed example showing exactly how powerful the pension tax breaks are and how you could end up with twice as much money as someone who invests outside a pension.

We then move on to a brief overview of the most interesting of the 'A-Day' pension rules, which came into operation on April 6th 2006. After this comes a detailed look at what types of property qualify for inclusion in a self-invested pension.

You may recall Gordon Brown's famous U-turn in December 2005, banning residential property from pensions. As it turns out, the legislation is not so bad after all and there are lots of property investments that still qualify.

Part 4 contains examples comparing bricks and mortar property investments with property ISAs and SIPPs. We also conduct a detailed comparison of ISAs and SIPPs to see which of these tax shelters is likely to leave you with most money at the end of the day.

Finally, Part 5 contains a few extra titbits, including how to save extra tax every year by using your ISA allowance in conjunction with your annual capital gains tax exemption.

Part 1

Property ISAs

A Simple and Tax-efficient Way to Invest

Chapter 1

Introduction to Property ISAs

The Individual Savings Account, or ISA, is one of very few tax shelters available to private investors in the UK. Others include pension funds, venture capital trusts and enterprise investment schemes.

ISAs don't enjoy as many tax breaks as other tax shelters – in particular, they don't give you an income tax refund when you put your money in.

What makes ISAs more attractive than other tax shelters is their *flexibility*:

- **No minimum investment period**. Your investment returns are completely tax free whether you invest for one day or one decade.

- **Easy access to your money**. You can leave your capital invested and withdraw income tax free at any time, or sell your investments and take a tax-free lump sum. Your ISAs are therefore both a tax-free savings vehicle and a tax-free income generator.

A few years ago there were fears ISAs would be scrapped altogether but in December 2006 the Government announced that these wonderful tax shelters will be around indefinitely.

And then in the April 2009 Budget the investment limit was raised from £7,200 to £10,200 – from 6th October 2009 for those aged 50+ and from 6th April 2010 for everyone else.

Hopefully the investment limit will be increased regularly to compensate for inflation. Even if this doesn't happen, it's still generous enough to help you build up a substantial tax-free nest egg. For example, over five years a couple can shelter up to £102,000 from the taxman plus all their investment income and profits.

Stock Market Turmoil

ISAs generally fell out of favour following the stock market collapse of 2000 to 2003. Sheltering profits from the taxman became the least of investors' worries... just making a profit in the first place seemed to take a miracle!

From April 2003 the stock market started rising strongly and ISAs came back into vogue.

And then it all started to unravel again. Between July 2007 and February 2009 the FTSE-100 fell from around 6,700 to 3,800 – a collapse of 43%.

It's hardly surprising that so many people are now completely disillusioned with stock market investing. If you invested in early 1996, you would not have made a single penny of profit by 2009 – some 13 years later!

The two massive stock market meltdowns which have taken place in the first decade of this century have completely debunked the conventional wisdom that shares always perform well in the long run.

Investing in Property

But ISAs aren't just for share investors. They can also be used to invest in certain types of property.

Property ISAs have been available for quite a few years now but did not receive much attention from the mainstream financial media in the early days. As a result, most investors were unaware of their existence.

In 2006 ISA investors were given the green light to invest in property unit trusts for the first time and a wall of money poured into the most popular funds.

January 2007 saw the much anticipated introduction in the UK of real estate investment trusts (REITs). These property investments can also be sheltered inside an ISA.

Of course, REITS and other property funds have not been immune from the wealth destruction which accompanied the credit crunch and the recession that resulted. Far from it.

Apart from banks, probably the worst performing stock market companies have been those in the real estate sector, in particular real estate investment trusts.

The share prices of many REITs – which are some of the UK's biggest landlords – have performed even worse than many of the internet companies whose share prices were decimated when the infamous Dot Com Bubble burst.

Nevertheless investing in property is still extremely popular and many shrewd investors are starting to see opportunities despite the general gloom and doom. That is why we have published this guide.

In this part I'm going to explain exactly how you go about investing in a property ISA, weigh up all their benefits and drawbacks and then take a detailed look at some of the investments available. I'm also going to explore other important issues that will be of interest to anyone investing in ISAs, not just property investors.

Every year some of the leading investment magazines publish ISA supplements. Most contain a list of expert share and unit trust tips and background information on how ISAs work. The better guides also contain detailed performance tables to help you choose the best investment funds for your ISA wrapper.

However, over the years I have found that none of the articles published in newspapers, magazines or specialist ISA supplements answers the *really* important questions. For example, instead of an ISA are you better off using your savings to invest somewhere else or to pay off your mortgage? Should you use an ISA to save for future expenses such as a child's education, or is it better to leave your savings intact to provide tax-free retirement income?

These are some of the questions to which I *personally* wanted concrete answers and hence I decided to do the research myself.

What you will not find here, however, are any specific investment recommendations.

Market timing is a fool's game and I have no idea whether property prices will rebound or fall further in the months ahead.

Professional property fund managers seem to agree that the prime end of the commercial property market has stabilised and point to growing demand from both big institutions and small private investors. Prices for secondary property are still falling, however.

Many property investments currently have very high income yields. For example, many of the REITs and stock exchange quoted property funds have seen their share prices take such a beating that they are now sitting on income yields of 10% or more. (Remember the income yield is calculated by dividing a fund's income distribution by its share price, so the lower the share price the higher the income yield).

If you are an optimist you can treat these high income yields as a screaming buy signal because property fund share prices are cheap.

If you are a pessimist you can argue that these income yields will fall, not because share prices will rise, but because the income distributions will be cut if the underlying property portfolios struggle to generate rental income.

Plummeting rental income now seems to be the biggest fear of property fund managers. In most big cities hundreds of shops are empty and there is a glut of office space, especially in London.

Tenants are using their bargaining power to force landlords to cut rents. In other cases they are simply going bust.

This dire situation could continue until 2010 or even beyond.

So while some property funds have high yields, they are not necessarily sustainable. You have to look for funds with a long average lease length and high dividend cover (the rental income should comfortably cover the income paid to investors).

For example, a fund with just 110% dividend cover could be forced to cut its income distribution if some of its tenants go bankrupt or if expiring leases cannot be renewed.

Chapter 2

Brand New Property Tax Shelters

Property ISAs are available from some of the UK's most reputable investment companies, such as Aviva, Axa, and Standard Life.

They're ideal for anyone wanting to invest in commercial property without the hassle of personally managing a portfolio of properties. They're also suitable for anyone who wants to maximize investment income.

The benefits are potentially huge. You get to invest in what is unquestionably the country's most popular type of asset – property – using what is arguably the cheapest and most flexible type of tax shelter.

So What Exactly is a Property ISA?

Let me start by explaining what I do NOT mean when I use the phrase 'property ISA'.

First of all, I do not mean buying actual bricks and mortar and sheltering them inside an ISA. Revenue & Customs regulations prevent you from investing in 'real' or 'actual' property.

As you'll see later on, however, property ISAs have a number of advantages over traditional bricks-and-mortar investments and are therefore a useful addition to most well-balanced investment portfolios.

Secondly, when I use the phrase property ISA I am not talking about *residential* property. At present most property ISAs are *commercial* property investments. This is both a benefit and a drawback. The commercial and residential property markets are quite separate – one can be rising when the other is falling.

Thirdly, property ISAs are not investments in general property companies such as stock-market-listed estate agents, construction companies, home builders and other organisations providing property services. Examples include the likes of Savills and Persimmon.

It's possible to put all of those property companies in an ISA and protect yourself from income tax and capital gains tax.

However, it's not these investments I'm referring to when I talk about property ISAs.

Property Funds

When I use the term property ISA I am referring specifically to **property funds**. A property fund is simply a pot of money used to buy a spread of buildings which are rented out.

Property funds are referred to as *indirect* property investments – the investor does not own the property itself. Instead he or she owns units or shares in a fund that owns property.

Property funds are the closest you will get to putting bricks and mortar in an ISA. The fund takes your money and sticks it directly into shopping centres, retail parks, offices and warehouses.

If everything goes to plan you will enjoy capital growth and a steady flow of rental income.

There are three types of property fund you can stick in an ISA:

- Property unit trusts
- Real estate investment trusts (REITs)
- Property investment companies

We'll take a closer look at each type of fund in Part 2. For now we'll just cover the basics.

Property Unit Trusts

Property unit trusts have been around for many years and some, such as Aviva Property Trust, have over £1 billion of property under management.

Property unit trusts take money from investors and use it to buy a spread of offices, high street shops, shopping centres, warehouses and factories.

For a small initial investment of usually no more than £1,000 the investor ends up owning a little piece of dozens of properties.

In return the fund management company charges a small annual fee.

You'll find property unit trust prices quoted in the *Financial Times* or on certain investment websites such as Trustnet.com.

Real Estate Investment Trusts (REITs)

REITs do pretty much the same job as property unit trusts: they own a big portfolio of properties, collect the rent and pay it out to shareholders.

There are, however, two important differences between REITs and property unit trusts:

- REITs are listed on the stock market (this has both benefits and drawbacks).

- REITs are allowed to borrow money, unit trusts cannot.

There are currently 21 REITs in the UK, the biggest being British Land and Land Securities. You'll find them quoted in the *Financial Times* on the 'London Share Service' pages under 'Real Estate'.

Another excellent source of REIT information is www.reita.org.

In Part 2, I'll take a more detailed look at the pros and cons of REITs and property unit trusts.

Property Investment Companies

Before 2006 the only way to invest in property through an ISA was to invest in a 'property investment company'. Like REITs, property investment companies are stock market listed and normally borrow to invest.

They're usually based offshore in the Channel Islands which brings certain benefits.

Although they don't market themselves aggressively or attract much press coverage they're managed by very reputable financial institutions such as Standard Life and Axa.

You'll find 'Investment Companies' at the end of the 'London Share Service' pages in the *Financial Times*.

An Example Fund

Let's take a very quick look at just one of the funds on offer so you have some idea what a property ISA actually looks like.

Take, for example, the Property Income Trust, a property investment company managed by life insurance giant Standard Life.

This fund has a portfolio of approximately 30 properties worth £160 million dotted around the UK, with 23% in offices and office parks, 15% in retail, 10% in leisure properties and 25% in distribution warehouses, industrial parks and standard industrial properties. A sizeable 28% of the portfolio is currently held in cash.

The fund is structured as a closed-ended Guernsey registered investment company. You'll find the share price online if you go to Yahoo Finance (uk.finance.yahoo.com) and type 'SLI' in the share price lookup box.

The shares have fallen from 140p back in 2006 to 45p at the time of writing – a fall of almost 70%.

The fund manager, a chap called Jason Baggaley, spends his days looking for new properties to invest in and selling properties that he thinks will fall in value or produce unattractive rental income. A recent acquisition was the purchase of a 54,000 sqft office in Uxbridge for £11 million at a yield of almost 10%.

When he's not doing that he'll be managing the existing portfolio: finding new tenants and negotiating new leases with existing ones.

For these services Standard Life receives an annual fee – 0.85% of assets under management.

Rents are collected and then paid out to investors as dividends. At present this fund pays an income of 4p per share. When you consider that shares in the fund cost 45 pence each, the 'rental yield' is 9%.

If you invest in the fund through an ISA that 9% income will, of course, be completely tax free. Because many property investors pay 40% income tax on their rental profits, that 9% is equivalent to earning 15% from a 'bricks and mortar' or direct property investment!

In other words, if you invest in commercial property outside an ISA you will have to earn a 15% rental yield to beat a fund like this held inside an ISA.

It's also critical to point out that 15% is *net of all costs*: interest on borrowings, management fees and so on.

A net rental yield of this magnitude is almost unheard of in the world of buy-to-let flats.

However, the income is by no means guaranteed and could fall if voids in the underlying properties increase significantly.

Every few months the portfolio is revalued and when these figures are published this will usually cause the shares to move up or down.

Like all quoted property funds the performance in recent years has been dismal. However, the shares have risen by almost 73% from the rock-bottom lows reached in March 2009.

At the time of writing the shares were trading at a discount of around 14% to their net asset value. We'll discuss the importance of discounts later on.

The Standard Life fund's main focus is to hold a diversified UK commercial property portfolio but it can also undertake property development up to 10% of its assets.

Many REITs are also involved in some property development but property unit trusts are usually not.

The Standard Life fund is allowed to borrow money to buy extra property and boost its rental income and capital growth. Most property investment companies and REITs do this which boosts their performance when property prices are going up but punishes returns when prices are falling.

Property unit trusts do not have any borrowings and as a result their prices have fallen less heavily during the recent property market collapse. Conversely, when a recovery eventually takes place, they will probably also not deliver returns as high as funds which have borrowings.

At present the Standard Life fund has a loan to value ratio of 39% which means that for every £1 of property, 39p is debt and 61p is owned outright (like the equity in a buy-to-let property).

If you want to buy shares in a fund like this all you have to do is phone up a stockbroker and you'll own them in minutes. However, to get the tax relief you have to buy them through an ISA, typically a self-select ISA. A self-select ISA is essentially a 'do-it-yourself' ISA, available from most major stockbrokers and other investment companies. They allow you to invest your money pretty much as you please (see Chapter 22 for more information on self-select ISAs).

Summary

- Property ISAs are not investments in 'direct property' or bricks and mortar.

- Property ISAs are investments in property unit trusts, REITs and property investment companies.

- These funds invest directly in commercial property. The properties earn rental income that is paid out to investors.

- A typical property ISA will invest in a spread of commercial properties dotted all over the UK (some funds are also starting to look further afield).

- A typical spread consists of shops, offices and industrial property. Some funds focus more on a specific sector, such as London offices or industrial properties.

- Some of these funds deliver a high income – up to 9% per year or more. Because ISA income is tax free this is equivalent to earning over 15% outside an ISA, net of all property costs. Very few bricks and mortar properties have *net* rental yields of 15%.

- All capital gains are completely tax free.

Chapter 3

How to Earn 80% More from Your Property Investments

Introduction

In the best-case scenario an ISA will protect 40% of your returns from the taxman. In the worst-case scenario you won't save any tax at all.

For example, an ISA probably won't necessarily save you much capital gains tax. This may come as a surprise to many readers but, thanks to a variety of reliefs and exemptions, most property fund investors can drastically reduce their capital gains tax or avoid it altogether, even without the help of an ISA.

ISAs are, however, fantastic **income tax shelters**. This is because income is generally taxed much more heavily than capital gains.

Take rental income, for example. There aren't any reliefs or exemptions to protect you as there are for capital gains tax purposes.

As a result higher-rate taxpayers normally pay the maximum 40% tax on all their rental profits.

Clearly anyone who wants to earn rental income has a lot to gain by investing in a tax-free property ISA – your disposable income will be significantly higher as a result.

In summary, if you want to make the most of your ISAs and enjoy big tax savings you have to choose your strategy very carefully.

That's what this chapter is all about.

Saving for Future Expenses

Many investors use ISAs to save for future expenses. For example, you may wish to accumulate funds to pay for something important like a child's university or private school education, or something fun like an overseas trip.

Saving for future expenses implies that you plan to cash in your ISAs at some point in the next, say, three to ten years.

At first glance this seems like a perfectly sensible strategy. In reality, it's not the most tax efficient way to use your ISA allowance, especially if you are investing in assets that are normally subject to capital gains tax, such as property funds. In many cases, you will not save one penny in CGT.

Example 1

Gordon and Sarah invest £5,000 <u>directly</u> in a property unit trust (note, not using an ISA) to help pay for their son's future university fees. Let's say they enjoy capital growth of 7% per year for 10 years and end up with a profit of £4,800 after selling their units.

These profits will be completely tax free because they're covered by the couple's annual capital gains tax exemptions (currently £10,100 per person per year).

So if Gordon and Sarah invested in the same unit trust but used an ISA wrapper instead, they would not save one penny in capital gains tax.

What if the couple invested much more money or earned a far higher return? Even in this situation an ISA may not be much use.

Example 2

Let's say Gordon and Sarah contribute £40,000 to ISAs over a few tax years and again earn 7% per year for 10 years. In this case they'll make a profit of almost £39,000 after a decade.

However, quite a lot of their profits will be protected from tax by their annual CGT exemptions. The CGT exemption rises with inflation so in 10 years' time it could be around £14,000, or £28,000 for a married couple.

So of Gordon and Sarah's £39,000 profits only £11,000 is taxable. The new capital gains tax rate is 18% so their total tax bill is £1,980.

In this example an ISA has saved the couple a fair amount of capital gains tax. However, even if they didn't use an ISA they could have avoided paying any capital gains tax by simply selling some of their investments in another tax year, thereby using two years worth of CGT exemptions.

There are, however, situations in which investors will always end up paying tax and will therefore always save money by using an ISA. The maximum tax savings are achieved when you use your ISAs for:

- Income, or
- Regular savings

ISAs for Income

The best thing to do with your ISAs is never sell them because, once you do that, the tax savings are lost forever. A better idea is to hold on to them and use the money to generate *tax-free income*.

Example 3

Gordon and Sarah invest £14,000 for 10 years in a growth ISA and enjoy returns of 7% per year. This time, however, the investment will not be cashed in and will, instead, be used to generate income.

After 10 years the investment will be worth £27,540 and they can switch tax free from the growth fund to an income-focused fund (ISA supermarkets, for example, let you invest in different funds provided by different managers and switch from one to another at low cost).

If the income fund has a yield of, say, 6% this will produce a tax-free income of £1,652 per year.

Now let's introduce William and Kate. They invest exactly the same amount as Gordon and Sarah but do <u>not</u> use an ISA. When they switch their funds 10 years later from growth investments to income-producing assets, they will be subject to capital gains tax. However, there won't be any tax to pay because their profits will be easily covered by their annual CGT exemptions.

However, that's not the end of the story. When the income fund starts paying out, the full amount will be subject to income tax, possibly at the rate of 40%. This will leave them with an after-tax income of just £991.

In other words, by using an ISA, Gordon and Sarah end up with almost 67% more income than William and Kate.

What's more, these tax savings will be enjoyed by the couple *every year*.

Clearly ISAs are a fantastic way of accumulating savings to generate income.

ISAs for Regular Savings

In the first example Gordon and Sarah didn't need to use an ISA – their profits were small enough to be fully covered by their annual CGT exemptions.

However, if you use your ISA allowance every year as part of a regular long-term savings programme you will eventually accumulate a significant amount of money and an ISA could save you a significant amount of tax.

Example 4

*Let's say Gordon and Sarah from the earlier example invest £14,000 **per year** for 15 years in an ISA. We'll assume the portfolio grows by 8% per year.*

At the end of the investment period the couple will end up with an impressive £410,540.

Because they've used an ISA there will, of course, be no capital gains tax on their profits and the full amount will be theirs to do with as they please. If they had invested <u>outside</u> an ISA there would be capital gains tax to pay when the investment was sold, calculated as follows:

Profit*	*£200,540*
Less: CGT Exemptions**	*£30,000*
Taxable Profit	*£170,540*
Tax @18%	*£30,697*
Remaining after tax	*£379,843*

* £410,540 minus 15 investments of £14,000.

** An estimate of two CGT exemptions in 15 years' time.

So using an ISA in this instance has definitely been worthwhile as the couple will save approximately £31,000 in capital gains tax. Had the couple not used an ISA it would have been more difficult, though not impossible, to sell their investment over many tax years to make use of their annual CGT exemptions.

ISAs for Income Revisited

The example earlier showed that the biggest tax savings are produced when you use your ISAs to generate tax-free income. In that example Gordon and Sarah earned 67% more income because they sheltered inside an ISA. It's an interesting result but they can still do better. Let's examine how much more income Gordon and Sarah earn by sheltering their regular savings from the above example in an ISA.

We've already shown that if they use an ISA they will end up with £410,540. They could then switch tax free into high-income assets paying, say, 6% tax free – an income of £24,632 per year.

If they invest *outside* an ISA they will have only £379,843 to invest for income after paying £30,697 in capital gains tax. This will produce an income of just £13,674:

£379,843 x 6% income – 40% income tax = £13,674

In other words, by saving with an ISA they will end up with an income of £24,632. Outside an ISA they will end up with just £13,674.

Investing through an ISA produces 80% more income.

This example shows ISAs at their most powerful: when used to generate tax-free income.

None of our assumptions are implausible. All we've assumed is that a couple make full use of their ISA allowance for 15 years and earn a respectable return of 8% per year.

Summary

- Saving for future expenses, such as a child's education, is possibly the worst way to use your ISA allowance. In many cases you will not save one penny in capital gains tax.

- Possibly the best thing to do with your ISAs is never sell them – instead use your savings to generate tax-free income. You could end up with 80% more income than someone who invests outside an ISA.

- If you invest your entire allowance each year and hold your investments for a long period of time you could also save a significant amount of capital gains tax by using an ISA.

Part 2

Property Funds

The Building Blocks of Property ISAs & SIPPs

Chapter 4

Property Funds: The Benefits

"A professionally managed, broadly diversified, liquid property portfolio, available for lump sum investments of only £1,000 is totally different from a single, speculative, and often highly geared, property asset." Gerardine Davies, manager of Aegon's £2 billion property portfolio.

Property has made a lot of people very wealthy in the last 10 years or so. When prices were rising by over 20% per year, anyone who borrowed to the limit and went on a spending spree would have made hundreds of thousands of pounds, if not millions.

However, there have been numerous casualties as well, in particular investors who purchased over-priced, newly built city centre apartments and all those who simply jumped on the bandwagon too late, just before property prices crashed.

Nevertheless, property investment is far from dead and many investors believe now is the time to start buying again. If you buy real estate in the right location and, critically, at the right price, it should grow in value over the years and produce a decent rental income.

You won't get rich quickly but you could grow rich *over time*.

Direct vs Indirect Property Investment

Direct investment means you own actual bricks and mortar, indirect investment means buying shares or units in a fund that owns bricks and mortar. That fund could be a unit trust, REIT or property investment company. Or it could be a much smaller and less formal arrangement among a group of investors.

Property funds address many of the problems of direct property ownership: they provide you with risk diversification (a big spread of properties), liquidity (you can usually buy and sell whenever you want) and expert management (property professionals who hunt down the best deals and squeeze as much rental income out of the properties as possible).

Furthermore, because the minimum investment in many funds is so low (no more than £1,000 in many cases) there is no requirement to use borrowed money. This should appeal to risk-averse investors or those struggling to obtain a mortgage deposit.

And if you invest through an ISA or pension your returns will be completely tax free!

In the next two chapters I'm going to take a detailed look at the benefits and drawbacks of investing in property funds compared with direct 'bricks-and-mortar' investments.

It's important to stress that there is no right or wrong way to invest in property, only what works well for YOU. Furthermore, it's not an all-or-nothing decision. You can invest some money in a property ISA and some in traditional bricks and mortar (and some in property pensions, as we'll see later).

Property ISAs offer both tax benefits and non-tax benefits. In my opinion the non-tax benefits are just as important.

Advantage #1 - Tax-Free Rental Income

We've already shown that an ISA can produce 67% more income than another taxed investment.

A more sophisticated way to compare property held inside an ISA with property held outside an ISA is to look at the long-term position with rental income being reinvested year after year.

Remember ISA investors can reinvest their income tax free whereas other property investors can only reinvest their after-tax income. This can make a big difference over a period of many years.

In fact, one of the drawbacks of traditional property investing is that it is very difficult to reinvest your income at all. For example, if you own a small property that produces income of £700 per month you will find it very difficult, if not impossible, to immediately reinvest that money in new property.

A major benefit of investing in a property ISA, or any investment fund for that matter, is that it is relatively easy to reinvest your income. This is because the minimum investment is so low and many funds have an automatic reinvestment facility.

Reinvesting income over a long period of time can have a significant effect on your overall investment returns.

Example 1

John, a higher-rate taxpayer has ISA savings of £20,000. Let's say he invests these in a property fund and enjoys capital growth of 5% per year and income of 5% per year. If he reinvests the tax-free income, after 10 years he will have an investment worth around £52,000.

If instead he invests in property outside an ISA he will have to pay tax on his rental income distributions and will therefore have less to reinvest. In fact his £20,000 initial investment will grow to just £43,000.

This example shows how ISAs are powerful wealth accumulators.

Example 2

John now decides to start spending his investment income. Because his money is in an ISA he can pay himself a tax-free income at any time. In this case his income will be:

$$£52,000 \times 5\% = £2,600$$

If he had invested outside an ISA his income would be:

$$£43,000 \times 5\% \text{ less } 40\% \text{ tax} = £1,290.$$

The ISA produces over twice the income after 10 years!

This example shows how ISAs are also powerful income generators.

Advantage #2 - Tax-free Capital Growth

When you sell shares in a property ISA you don't have to pay one penny of capital gains tax (CGT).

If you sell property investments held *outside* an ISA you are subject to capital gains tax.

Bricks and mortar commercial property often used to qualify for business asset taper relief which meant investors only paid tax at 10% on their profits.

Since April 2008 commercial property investors have seen their tax rate jump to 18%.

So holding commercial property investments in a tax-free wrapper such as an ISA has become even more attractive following the recent change to capital gains tax.

Advantage #3 - Property Funds Are Liquid

This is an important advantage of property funds over traditional property. The more liquid an investment is, the better.

Just ask anyone who has struggled for many months to sell a property. While you wait for a buyer you have to pay mortgage interest, council tax, insurance and other running costs and will probably not be earning a penny in rental income.

Most bricks and mortar property is extremely illiquid because you cannot sell it quickly, unless you accept a drastic drop in price.

Property funds generally do not suffer from this problem. For example, REITs can be sold within minutes by phoning your stockbroker or clicking a mouse if you have an online share-dealing account.

Unit trusts can also be cashed in quickly by contacting the fund management company in question. This is certainly the case during normal market conditions. However, during periods of market panic, property unit trusts can be as difficult to sell as bricks and mortar property investments.

In 2007 many property unit trust investors started selling because they were worried about a crash in commercial property prices. It quickly transpired that most of the property unit trusts did not have enough cash to meet a large number of redemptions. This meant they had to start a fire sale of properties – a process that can take many months.

To put investors off selling, many funds started levying an exit penalty of up to 7% and some even placed a complete block on redemptions.

So the lesson to be learned is that, while most property funds are more liquid than bricks and mortar property, some property funds are more liquid than others. Those such as REITs which are quoted on the stock exchange are extremely liquid, whereas property unit trusts can be extremely illiquid during times of market upheaval.

Selling Part of Your Investment

Bricks-and-mortar property is also illiquid in the sense that you cannot sell it off in chunks. For example, you would struggle to sell 20% of a buy-to-let flat but you would not struggle to sell 20% of your shares in a REIT.

In fact, the ability to sell off your investment in chunks is also extremely useful if you're investing without the protection of an ISA. By selling off small parcels of shares or unit trusts each year, investors can make use of their annual capital gains tax (CGT) exemptions much more readily than direct property investors.

Very few direct property investors can make use of their CGT exemption every year because the costs incurred buying and selling property are too prohibitive.

Example

Lee has shares that have made a profit of £18,000. Instead of selling them all in one go he decides to sell half his holding at the end of the current tax year and the remaining half at the beginning of the new tax year.

As a result, all of his profit will be tax free because the first £9,000 in profit will be covered by this year's annual CGT exemption and the second £9,000 will be covered by next year's annual exemption.

If Lee owned a property with an £18,000 profit he would probably have to sell the whole asset in one go. The first £10,100 would be covered by his annual CGT exemption. The tax bill on the remaining £7,900 would be £1,422.

Advantage #4 - Big Spread of Properties

This is without doubt one of the major attractions of property funds over direct property investment. Commercial property is usually a lot more expensive than residential property so most investors cannot afford to invest in a broad range of sectors and in a broad range of geographic locations.

In fact, most residential property investors also cannot afford to spread their risk by buying lots of different properties in different locations.

Putting your money in a property fund means you can invest in a property portfolio worth, say, £300 million with assets spread all over the country and divided among shops, offices and industrial units.

Just imagine owning part of a £10 million office block in the centre of London, a £15 million shopping centre in Manchester and a £9 million industrial park near Birmingham... plus dozens more properties like these spread all over the country.

Spreading risk is usually not a top priority for most property investors. Many have huge sums of money tied up in just a handful of properties. It's usually only when problems arise that the investor wishes he hadn't put so many eggs into one basket.

For example, if you only own one property and cannot find a tenant for, say, 12 months, that could cause you serious financial hardship if you have a mortgage to cover or depend on the rent to pay your living expenses.

Having two properties doesn't make matters much better.

However, if you own a small share in dozens of properties – as property fund investors often do – you don't have to worry if one or two are empty for any length of time.

There are lots of other problems that may arise if a lot of your wealth is tied up in just one or two properties. Apart from rental voids there are literally hundreds of other factors – unknown at the time you purchase the property – that could have an adverse effect on the rental income you receive or the capital growth of the property.

For example, if the property is badly flooded it may be impossible to rent out for several months. If the property has structural damage that was not discovered when the survey was carried out, it may cost thousands of pounds to rectify. If the area where the property is located becomes undesirable this will severely affect rental and capital values.

If you still think spreading your risk is not important you should heed the warning of David Pearl, a very experienced property investor whose story I read recently. One of his buildings, a recently empty office block in London, had just been refurbished at considerable cost when the local council approved a builder's plan to redevelop the area.

This meant the building could become the subject of a compulsory purchase order. Such orders often take years to unravel and in the meantime the investor is left with a building that can neither be rented out nor sold.

Pearl brought his story to the attention of readers of *Property Week* magazine: "...Imagine if you were an investor owning only one building, which you hoped would provide you with a pension. It might represent your life savings. You bought it hoping that it would provide you with a good income then suddenly the rent tap is turned off."

Something like this could happen to anyone. In this case the building was just one part of a big portfolio so the overall effect was minimal. The lesson to be learned from horror stories such as this is: if you cannot afford to buy a big portfolio of properties, one way of spreading your risk is to invest in a property fund.

Advantage #5 - No Borrowings Required

Property funds require a small outlay so no borrowings are necessary. You can invest as little as £100 whereas the deposit alone on a direct property is usually 200 times that amount.

There are some investment companies promoting 'no money down' deals that do not require deposits but, in my experience, these are difficult to arrange, particularly now that banks have tightened their lending criteria. Because only small investments are required, property funds are also ideally suited to a regular monthly savings plan.

Furthermore, because most bricks and mortar property investors have to borrow money this exposes them to a variety of risks. Many experienced investors argue that property itself is not risky (at least not in the long run), it's the borrowings that create the problems. Borrowing exposes you to:

- **Interest rate risk**. If interest rates go up you may not be able to meet the cost of your borrowings out of your rental income, which means you will have to rely on other income sources to pay your debt.

- **Rental voids**. Residential property leases usually last for 12 months or less. This means your property stands a good chance of being empty for *at least* one month in 12. During these periods, which can last many months in areas swamped with buy-to-let property, you still have to find the funds to pay your mortgage and other expenses. Commercial property leases usually last much longer but when a lease comes to an end it may take many months, sometimes years, to find replacement tenants.

- **Reverse Gearing**. If property prices fall your deposit will bear the full brunt of the fall. The following example illustrates this point.

34

Example

The Paltrows and the Therons each have £14,000 to invest. The Paltrows invest £14,000 in a property fund, whereas the Therons use their money as a deposit on a small buy-to-let property costing around £94,000.

Property prices fall by just 5%. How much does each couple lose? The Paltrows' total investment is just £14,000 so they lose 5% of their money, which is just £700. The Therons' total property investment is £94,000 so they lose £4,700, which is a whopping 33% of their personal money (their deposit).

Clearly, any drop in property values hits investors who have mortgages far harder than investors who do not.

Having said that it's important to bear in mind that many property funds themselves borrow significant amounts of money. Property unit trusts are generally restricted from borrowing but REITs and other stock exchange quoted property companies are often heavily geared.

So when property prices fall a geared property fund will fall sharply too. If property prices fall far enough the fund could breach its bank covenant which means it will be forced to sell properties to repay debt.

Many property funds have found themselves in this situation in the last two years. For example, in 2007 Invesco Property Income came perilously close to breaking its bank covenants and was forced to start selling properties.

As a result the shares collapsed from 87p to 31p in the space of just a few weeks.

In summary, investing in property funds does not expose you to the monthly mortgage commitments of buy to let investors but could leave you exposed to a fall in property prices.

Advantage #6 - Help in Troubled Times

Property ISA investments can help you in times of financial hardship. For example, if you lose your job you could use savings accumulated in an ISA to pay your bills for several months.

Even if you don't need to draw on your savings, you can simply stop making any new investments and rest assured that your ISAs will provide no additional financial burden.

Direct property investment, on the other hand, often depends on you being in tip-top financial health.

For example, if a property is empty for any period you will have no rental income to pay the mortgage, insurance and repairs and will also be liable for council tax or business rates.

Even if the property is fully occupied it could still be a drain on your finances if the rental income does not cover all the costs.

So if you lose your primary source of income, for example, if you're made redundant or your business goes bust, your direct property investments could continue to provide an unwelcome drain on your cash flow.

Advantage #7- Low Upfront Charges

Investors usually have to pay upfront charges when they invest in any kind of asset, be it property or shares.

The good news for property fund investors is that these charges are usually very low: normally less than 1% of the amount invested. Property unit trusts have higher upfront charges – usually 5% – but these can be easily reduced or avoided if you invest through one of the unit trust supermarkets.

Direct property upfront charges are far less predictable. They vary from investor to investor and between residential and commercial property. There could be legal fees, survey fees, mortgage arrangement fees, stamp duty of up to 4%, mortgage interest payments prior to letting, refurbishment and decorating costs, furniture and white good investments and letting agent registration fees.

In total you could end up paying up to 7% of the property's value in upfront charges. The important point to remember is that, as a percentage of your *personal investment* – your deposit – direct property upfront costs are much greater... more in the region of 30%.

So if you decided to sell a property soon after purchasing it, the costs are likely to eat up a large percentage of your personal stake in the property. Furthermore, when you sell a property you also have to pay estate agent's fees and legal fees again, which could easily come to an extra 2% to 3%. Property investment funds usually do not have significant exit costs.

Advantage #8 - No Personal or Hidden Costs

Property funds have annual fees of between 0.85% and 1.5% of the value of the properties under management. These aren't low but you don't have to pay this money *personally* – the fund manager simply knocks it off the value of your investment.

Ongoing charges for direct property investments are far more variable and often come out of your own pocket.

The *predictable* costs include letting agent's fees, building and contents insurance and accountant fees. The great thing about property funds, however, is that there are absolutely *no surprise costs*. When you invest in buy-to-let property you may find that your property and tenants make constant demands on your wallet.

These hidden costs are so great in number it's impossible to list them. Here are some of the most frustrating ones that I personally have had to pay for various properties in recent months:

- Repair creaking laminate – £90
- Damp proof walls – £1,500
- Replace washing machine after just 1 month – £200
- Emergency electrician – £60
- Re-attach radiator to wall – £60
- Repair flood damage caused by tenant – £100 excess

In case you're wondering what's so frustrating about having to foot the bill for an emergency electrician, it was so that the tenant could enjoy the privilege of having someone flick the fuse box switch back on after the power tripped!

These extra costs are the most exasperating aspect of buy-to-let.

You want to strangle your surveyor for not spotting any faults before you bought the property, you want to strangle your tenant for being so careless with your property and you want to strangle your letting agent for using such expensive tradesmen!

There's a good chance these expenses will eat up a significant percentage of your rental profits unless your mortgage payments are low.

With commercial property it's slightly different. For example, many leases require the tenant to pay insurance costs and maintain the building. However, when push comes to shove you can be sure that your building will not be maintained to a satisfactory level by someone else.

Advantage #9 - No Time Cost

Did I say that hidden expenses were the most exasperating part of property investing? I meant to say all the time it takes to manage them!

The point here is that *even if you use a letting agent* your direct property investments will probably still take up a lot of your time, especially if you're very ambitious and want to acquire a large portfolio. Letting agents are great at doing the mundane things like collecting rents but, in my experience, many are not very useful when you really need them.

Apart from all the day-to-day problems you may get dragged into as a property investor, you will also have to draw up accounts, which can be time consuming or expensive if you own lots of property. In my opinion, building a substantial property investment portfolio is not compatible with holding down a busy career or looking after a family.

As a property fund investor you have no time cost to worry about. Just like anyone who buys shares in any listed company or invests in a unit trust, you do not have to get involved in the day-to-day running of the company or fund.

Advantage #10 - Expert Management

If you invest in a property fund you will also benefit from having an experienced professional manage your investment. The experts who run these portfolios bring three major skills to the table:

- They have the expertise and information to scout out new properties offering above-average returns.

- They have the skills to identify which sectors (for example, shops or offices) are likely to deliver superior returns.

- They have the experience to negotiate new leases with tenants and ensure that every property produces the highest possible rental income.

However, I'm not going to get too carried away touting the virtues of professional property fund managers. To be honest, I am appalled at how badly most have coped with the recent downturn.

It would not be unreasonable to ask whether they are anything more than glorified janitors!

Many bought too many properties far too late in the cycle and used huge amounts of borrowed money to do it.

And most reacted far too slowly when things turned sour and were reluctant to start offloading the buildings in their portfolios.

The bottom line is that there are probably many readers who have been more skilful in managing the ups and downs of the property market than the full-time professionals.

Advantage #11 - Greater Flexibility

Property fund investors can chop and change their investments according to where the best returns are to be found.

For example, you could switch from one property fund with a heavy weighting in, say, shopping centres to another fund with a bigger concentration of regional offices.

If you invest in property funds via an ISA or SIPP you can do this without incurring any significant charges and without paying a penny in capital gains tax.

Direct property investors do not enjoy this amount of flexibility. If you own a flat in Manchester and you feel Manchester property prices are too high it could cost you an arm and a leg to sell up and buy a new property in, say, Birmingham.

You'll have to pay estate agent's fees and legal fees when you sell the Manchester property as well as capital gains tax on the remaining profits.

Then when you buy the new property in Birmingham you will have to pay another round of legal fees, stamp duty and maybe all the other upfront costs listed earlier.

The following example reveals how incredibly expensive it can be to sell one property in a low-growth area and buy a new one in a property hotspot.

Example

Dawn feels the Edinburgh property market is overpriced and decides to sell her flat for £150,000 so that she can reinvest the proceeds in Belfast.

She bought the property for £100,000 10 years ago. She paid for the property with a personal deposit of £15,000 and used an interest-only mortgage for the balance.

Her actual ownership of the property is therefore her £15,000 deposit plus her £50,000 profit, which comes to £65,000. She sells the property and after paying estate agent fees, legal fees and capital gains tax is left with just £54,000 of her own money.

After paying a fresh round of legal fees, mortgage fees, stamp duty and other costs she could only have around £50,000 of her own money to invest (her original £15,000 deposit and the leftover profits of £35,000 after all taxes and selling and buying costs have been deducted.)

So by simply switching from one property to another she has lost approximately 23% of her own money!

In summary, if you invest in property directly it is time consuming and expensive to shuffle your investments around and invest in new up-and-coming areas.

If you invest in a property fund it is easy, cheap and tax free to shuffle your investments around and rebalance your portfolio.

Advantage #12 - Transparent and Regulated

With unit trusts and stock exchange companies it's easy to monitor the performance of the investment over time. Share prices are printed daily in newspapers, for example, and are easily available on the internet.

REITs are governed by company law and stock-exchange rules, as well as certain accounting and corporate governance standards.

They also have boards of directors who are legally obliged to act in the interests of shareholders and to monitor investment performance and control costs on their behalf.

All this provides some protection for investors... but it does not protect you from poor investment decisions.

Summary

Property funds have the following benefits over direct property:

- **Tax-free rental income**. ISA investors can easily earn 67% more income than direct property investors and possibly 100% more income.

- **Tax-free capital gains**. This benefit is probably less important than the income tax savings but more important than in the past due to recent increases in capital gains tax for commercial property investors.

- **Liquidity**. Your investment can generally be bought or sold within minutes and sold off in small chunks.

- **Big spread of properties.** You can own a small share of dozens of office blocks, shopping centres and industrial parks, located all over the country.

- **No need for a mortgage.** Borrowing money is what makes property investment risky.

- **Help in troubled times.** You can sell your ISA savings quickly and use them to bail you out of financial difficulty. Traditional property investing requires you to be in tip-top financial health.

- **Low charges.** Property funds have low upfront charges, low ongoing charges and no hidden costs.

- **No time cost.** Property funds require virtually no time commitment from the investor, making them ideal for people with busy working lives or family commitments.

- **Expert management.** Property funds are managed by experienced property professionals who scour the country for new properties and try to maximize the rental income from existing properties.

- **Investment flexibility.** Property fund investors can sell existing investments and reinvest in alternative assets cheaply and without having to pay tax.

Chapter 5

Property Funds: The Drawbacks

Property funds are certainly not without drawbacks, however:

Drawback #1 - Less Gearing Benefit

You generally cannot borrow money to invest in property funds. In normal market conditions many investors will see this as a serious drawback because borrowing is the way to make big money in property when the market is rising. Even rich investors borrow money to give their returns a boost. Americans call this 'leverage' because it's the financial equivalent of using a lever to shift a boulder – you can achieve much more power than simply relying on your own resources.

Example

Jeffrey and Mary have £14,000 to invest. They use it as a deposit on a small flat costing £70,000 and borrow the rest of the money. Now let's assume the value of the property increases by 5% per year over the next 10 years.

We'll also assume that their rental income only covers the cost of their interest-only mortgage and their other letting costs – so all the couple are left with at the end of the day is the rise in the value of their property and their initial deposit.

After 10 years the property is worth £114,023. If they sell it and repay their £56,000 loan they'll be left with £58,023. What the couple have achieved, despite earning very modest returns, is to turn £14,000 into £58,023 in just 10 years. This means they have earned about 15% per year on their original money.

This ability to turn a 5% return into a 15% return is sometimes called the 'magic of gearing':

Even investments that earn modest returns can make you rich if you borrow money to invest in them.

As long as your investment returns exceed the cost of borrowing you should be OK.

There are, of course, big risks involved if you borrow money to invest in property. It's extremely unattractive when prices are falling.

Even if prices fall just a little, the value of your investment will fall a lot. And if property prices fall a lot you could be wiped out financially.

Property ISA investors cannot gear up their investments *personally*, however it's important to remember that some property funds gear up their portfolios using borrowed money. Property unit trusts are not allowed to do this but real estate investment trusts (REITs) can borrow as much money as private investors.

This gearing helped these companies boost their returns considerably up until the beginning of 2007 and also explains why they performed so badly in the months that followed.

In summary, direct property investors who borrow more money can enjoy higher returns than property fund investors... provided everything goes to plan: property prices rise, rental income covers mortgage repayments and interest rates stay low.

However, as we will see in Chapter 17, a property fund investor with no borrowings could, in certain circumstances, earn a higher return than a heavily geared buy-to-let investor.

Drawback #2 - Property Funds Can Be More Volatile

One of the things property investors hate most about the stock market is its horrendous volatility. There's nothing worse than turning on the 10 o'clock news and discovering that most of your wealth has been wiped out because Iceland forgot to pay its credit card bill.

Stock market investments are subject to vicious price swings that do not affect those who invest in other assets such as bricks and mortar property. And there's no getting away from the fact that some property funds (REITs and property investment companies) are stock market investments.

This means their prices change by the minute – sometimes by between 5 and 10 per cent.

In *theory*, stock exchange quoted property funds should not be affected by the ups and downs experienced by other company shares. This is because earnings from these companies are relatively predictable – they mostly earn rental income and much of that rental income is known for years into the future.

Earnings from other companies are much less predictable over long periods of time and based on, for example, how many units of software or cans of beer they can sell. Investment analysts find these numbers far more difficult to guess.

In *practice*, however, what most property investors are concerned about is the value of the properties in the portfolio and that is much harder to predict.

In 2007 shares in British Land, one of the biggest real estate investment trusts, plummeted by an astonishing 50%. This kind of price fall would leave most buy-to-let investors aghast.

The shares fell not because the net assets in the portfolio had actually fallen by 50% but because investors were worried that they might fall by this much in the months or even years ahead.

The stock market reacts far quicker and usually far more aggressively than the underlying property market. This can be very painful for existing investors thinking of selling but it can also open up significant buying opportunities if shares fall to bargain basement levels.

Property unit trusts are not quoted on the stock market and are therefore less vulnerable to this kind of volatility. However, they can suffer rapid price falls if investors are panic selling.

Drawback #3 - Discounts & Premiums

The share prices of stock exchange quoted property funds (REITs and property investment companies) are often significantly different to the underlying value of their property portfolios.

When this happens the funds are said to trade at a premium or a discount to net asset value.

Discounts and premiums do not apply to property unit trusts. The value of a typical unit trust is simply the value of the investments it owns.

With stock market funds it's slightly different. The investor buys shares in a company that owns properties. The company's share price is then determined by one thing and one thing only: investor demand.

If lots of investors want the shares the price will rise and if lots of investors want to dump the shares, the price will fall.

As a result, the price of the company's shares at any given point in time could be wildly different to its net asset value.

For example, if investors are extremely downbeat, the shares will be sold en masse, the price will fall and this will lead to the shares trading at a large discount.

In recent times many real estate investment trusts have traded at discounts of over 40%.

Does this mean the shares are cheap and worth buying? Sometimes, but not always.

Often the net asset value is unrealistic because the properties have not been valued for several months. If the properties are revalued and found to be worth much less than before, the discount will have been fully justified.

More importantly, when the property market is falling the funds that trade at the biggest discounts are usually the ones with the highest borrowings, ie the most risky. This reflects the market's fear that a significant amount of the equity in the portfolio could be wiped out if property prices continue falling.

When you buy shares in a property fund that borrows money you do not actually own properties. What you actually own is *equity* in properties. The equity is simply the value of the properties minus the borrowings.

As any experienced property investor knows, the equity in a property portfolio which has large borrowings can be wiped out by just a small fall in property prices.

For example, in the year to March 2009 British Land's property portfolio declined in value by 28%. However, because the company has significant borrowings its net asset value dropped by 64%.

This is why the share prices of stock market quoted property funds have traded at such large discounts in recent times. Investors have not been prepared to pay full price for a property portfolio which has excessive borrowings and could easily end up with negative equity, ie worthless.

So when you read articles in which journalists talk about property funds trading at 'attractive' discounts, remember it is not the properties themselves which are up for sale at a 40% discount, it is the *equity* in the portfolio and that portfolio could have extremely high borrowings.

When Big Discounts are a Buying Opportunity

Having said all that, property funds that trade at big discounts provide an opportunity to buy in at bargain prices, if the market recovers shortly afterwards. When markets recover, discounts tend to narrow, helping boost returns even further.

It's not uncommon, however, for discounts to persist for some time if there is very little investor confidence in a sector. This can be extremely frustrating for the investor who feels he has bought property assets on the cheap but is not enjoying any growth.

The crucial point is that, because share prices do not always mirror the underlying property portfolios, investors in quoted property funds like REITs often do not experience the same returns as bricks-and-mortar property investors.

This proves that quoted property funds are not 'true' property investments, especially over short periods of time. Over very long periods of time, however, most quoted property funds do trade quite close to their net asset values and the better managed ones sometimes trade at a premium.

Drawback #4 – Investment Limits

If you have a big lump sum you cannot invest in a property ISA – not in one go anyway. Currently the maximum annual investment is just £7,200 per person. Couples can invest £14,400. Starting on 6th April 2010, the investment limit rises to £10,200 for everyone.

The investment limit means that you will never be able to build vast amounts of wealth in an ISA. Over time, however, it is possible to accumulate a significant amount of money and shelter all the income and capital growth from the taxman.

For example, a couple who invest the maximum amount each year and enjoy investment returns of 7% per year will end up with £322,000 after five years and £513,000 after 15 years.

Drawback #5 - No Residential Property at Present

At present most property funds invest exclusively in *commercial property* and hold little or no residential property. The commercial and residential markets are completely different animals – one can be booming while the other is collapsing.

Many property investors, who own portfolios of buy-to-let flats, have very little knowledge of commercial property and absolutely no interest in dipping their toes into this market.

However, it could be argued that every well balanced investment portfolio should hold some commercial property and that property funds are the ideal route for inexperienced investors.

Before the recession started to bite many property experts used to argue that commercial property provides a far more reliable income stream than residential buy-to-let.

Most residential leases are of very short duration and tenants are usually private individuals, sometimes with little financial standing. Commercial property leases usually last for several years (five to 10 years) and your tenants could be big blue-chip companies.

However, many well-known high street companies have now gone bust (eg Woolworths) and landlords have found it extremely difficult to find replacement tenants.

The largest private residential landlord in the UK is a company called Grainger plc. Grainger owns around 25,000 properties and specialises in retirement homes and regulated tenancies (the tenant usually pays a lower rent and has lifetime occupation rights and in return Grainger buys the property at a discount).

Grainger's shares qualify for inclusion in an ISA or SIPP and your dividends and capital gains will be tax free. However, because the company is not a REIT it pays corporation tax on its income and capital gains. So putting the shares in an ISA or SIPP would protect you from paying tax *personally* but your investment would not be a proper tax shelter because the company will still be paying tax.

Grainger has not coped very well with the downturn in the property market. It recently made a loss and decided to defer its dividend. The company has a high loan to value ratio which means its bankers could force it to sell properties to raise cash. And, of course, now is not a great time to sell residential properties!

As we'll see in Chapter 15 there is also a growing number of unregulated funds that invest in residential property and qualify for inclusion in a self-invested personal pension (SIPP).

Drawback #6 - No Genuine Bargains

One of the advantages of direct property investment is that genuine bargains can be had, provided you spend time acquiring the necessary local knowledge. In other words, if you know what you're doing it's possible to find property selling for 'less that it should'.

This is rarely if ever possible with stock market investing. The stock market is a much more 'efficient' market than the property market. Being 'inefficient' makes the property market far more attractive to private investors.

Also, with property it's much easier to become an expert in one small area (for example, one type of property in one particular location) and reap significant rewards as a result. Having such 'insider knowledge' is one of the keys to making profitable property investments.

If you invest in a property fund you are not going to be picking up any amazing bargains (although it is possible to buy some stock exchange listed funds at a discount). Any capital growth you enjoy will be mainly due to a general rise in property prices rather than your skill at finding undervalued properties.

Drawback #7 - It Ain't Bricks & Mortar

There's no escaping the fact that property fund investors do not own actual bricks and mortar. Instead they end up with shares or units in a big company or unit trust.

Although you do own property, you only own it *indirectly*.

Financial advisors and property company executives often fail to appreciate the amount of passion many buy-to-let investors have for their properties and for doing deals.

If you invest in a property fund you will have no say in the management of the portfolio.

Chapter 6

Real Estate Investment Trusts: Answers to All Your Questions

REITs are simply stock market companies that own big portfolios of rental properties. They're relatively new to the UK investment scene so it's worth looking at their benefits and drawbacks in a bit of detail.

Before the introduction of REITs property companies suffered from *double taxation*: the company itself had to pay corporation tax on its rental income and capital gains and the investors had to pay income tax and capital gains tax on their dividends and profits.

Property companies that become REITs have to comply with a long list of rules but the reward is a 'get out of jail' card that frees them from ever having to pay tax on their rental properties again.

The investors still have to pay income tax on the rental income paid out by the REIT and capital gains tax when they sell their shares.

Property income distributions from REITs are taxed in the same way as rental profits from a buy-to-let property. In other words, basic-rate taxpayers have to pay 20% tax and higher-rate taxpayers pay tax at 40%.

The REIT itself deducts the first 20% and pays this money to the taxman. Higher-rate taxpayers then have to pay the extra 20% tax when they complete their tax returns.

However, the good news is that income distributions are paid without tax deducted when you invest through an ISA or SIPP.

REITs sometimes also pay dividends which are taxed in exactly the same way as any other company's dividends (and are also tax free in an ISA or SIPP).

When you sell REIT shares you also have to pay capital gains tax in the same way as when you sell ordinary buy-to-let property. However, if the shares are held inside an ISA or SIPP there is no CGT payable.

In conclusion, if you invest in REITs through a self-invested personal pension (SIPP) or ISA you have a property investment that is 100% tax free.

The REIT Rules

REITs have to comply with lots of rules to obtain these tax exemptions. Most of this red tape is of no interest to private investors. However, some of the rules shape the attractiveness of REITs to private investors:

- The company has to be a 'UK resident' and quoted on a 'recognised stock exchange' (in practice, the London Stock Exchange).

  This means REITs operate in a highly regulated environment that provides protection to investors but also means this type of property investment is likely to be more volatile than traditional bricks and mortar (see Chapter 5 on the drawbacks of listed property funds).

  The requirement of a stock exchange listing also prevents owners of small private property companies enjoying the REIT tax breaks.

- To become a REIT a property company has to pay a once-off conversion charge of 2% of its gross assets. Many companies believe this is a small price to pay for a lifetime tax exemption. Slough Estates claimed it would save £460 million in tax on capital gains, compared with the £78 million it had to pay in conversion charges.

- 90% of the company's rental profits have to be paid out to investors. The remaining 10% can be used to develop new properties.

- 75% of a REIT's income must come from property letting and 75% of its assets must be rental properties.

(The remaining 25% of its income can come from higher risk activities such as property trading and development – these activities are not tax exempt, however.)

- REITs are allowed to invest in residential property. However, there aren't any REITs specializing in the housing sector at present.

- REITs are allowed to have significant borrowings. Every £1 of interest paid has to be covered by £1.25 of rental profits. This level of gearing equates to a loan-to-value ratio of 80% – similar to the amount of borrowing to which most buy-to-let investors are accustomed.

  Of course, the higher a company's borrowings the less rental profit it will have to pay out. The focus will then be on generating capital growth.

REIT Benefits & Drawbacks

REITs are property funds so most of the pros and cons discussed in Chapters 4 and 5 apply.

For example, on the plus side REITs have the following advantages over direct bricks and mortar investments:

- Tax-free rental income and capital gains via an ISA or SIPP

- Liquidity – Your investment can be sold in minutes

- Big spread of properties

- No need to borrow to invest

- Very low buying and selling costs

- No time cost – the investment is completely passive

- Flexibility to switch from one REIT to another without having to pay tax

And on the negative side:

- REITs are more volatile than direct property

- REIT shares can trade at a premium or discount to the underlying properties

- No residential property REITs available at present

- No 'genuine bargains' in the REIT sector

How Do You Invest in REITs?

REITs are bought in exactly the same way that you buy shares in any stock market company: by phoning a stockbroker or using an online share dealing service.

ISA investors can buy them through a self-select ISA (see Chapter 22) and pension investors can buy them through their SIPPs (see Chapter 16).

Buying shares is far less costly than buying direct property. Stamp duty is just 0.5% and stockbrokers' dealing charges are extremely competitive these days.

The final cost is the 'dealing spread' – the difference between the buying price and the selling price of the shares. In stock market lingo these are known as the offer and bid prices respectively.

For example, at the time of writing Land Securities had a buying price of 422.75p and a selling price of 422.25p. So if you bought the shares and then sold them immediately you would lose just ½p per share owing to the spread.

These costs are very modest compared with those you rack up buying and selling bricks and mortar property.

Investing via a Fund

Another way to invest in REITs is via a unit trust or investment trust. These qualify for inclusion in ISAs and SIPPs so the investment will still be tax free.

The advantage of investing in a fund is that it allows you to invest in a big spread of REITs, both in the UK and abroad.

Many REITs, despite having big portfolios, are quite specialized. For example, some like Great Portland Estates focus on offices, others like Brixton focus on industrial properties and some, like Liberty International specialise in retail property.

Even the so-called diversified REITs, like Land Securities and British Land, are quite focused. For example, Land Securities has a £9 billion property portfolio but £5 billion of that is in London and almost 80% is offices.

The advantage of investing in REITs via a unit trust or investment trust is that you do not need specialist knowledge about which sectors (shops, offices or retail) or regions to invest in and you do not need to have any in-depth knowledge about the individual REITs – the fund manager does it all for you.

In return you will have to pay some charges but these are relatively modest. For example, the upfront and annual charges should be no more than 1%.

Unit trusts that invest heavily in UK REITs include Aberdeen Property Share Fund and Scottish Widows Investment Partnership UK Real Estate.

For more information about these and other funds go to trustnet.com.

Also note that most financial advisors know absolutely nothing about REITs and are not qualified to advise on these investments. REITs are the realm of stockbrokers, not IFAs.

Chapter 7

Directory of Real Estate Investment Trusts

There are currently 21 UK REITs. Some invest across sectors (eg, shops and offices) and all over the country. Others are more specialist and stick to one type of property and often one region. For example, Land Securities is a diversified REIT with a huge portfolio of offices and retail properties, Liberty specialises in shopping centres, Primary Health owns a portfolio of doctors' surgeries and Workspace rents out small offices and industrial units in London.

The following is a full listing. You'll find lots of extra information at www.reita.org and on the individual companies' websites:

Big Yellow Group

Big Yellow rents out self storage property in London and the South of England. It has now embarked on a UK-wide expansion plan.

www.bigyellow.co.uk

British Land

This is one of the two biggest REITs. Over half of the portfolio consists of retail properties, including approximately 200 retail warehouses and superstores. Almost 40% of the property is London offices and office developments, including Broadgate.

www.britishland.com

Brixton

Brixton manages a portfolio of more than 18 million sq ft of industrial properties and warehouse space. Most of the portfolio is located in the South East with a particular focus on the Heathrow and West London markets.

www.brixton.plc.uk

Derwent London
Derwent specialises in offices, in particular central London.

www.derwentlondon.com

Glenstone Property Group
Glenstone is one of the newest REITs with a portfolio totalling less than £100 million focused on market town retail properties throughout the UK. For example, a recent purchase was a £17 million portfolio of 11 shops in towns like Colchester, Scarborough and York.

www.glenstoneproperty.co.uk

Great Portland Estates
Great Portland Estates focuses on retail and offices in central London.

www.gpe.co.uk

Hammerson
Hammerson operates in both the UK and France. The group invests in and develops shopping centres, retail parks and offices.

www.hammerson.com

Highcroft Investments
Highcroft is a new and tiny REIT which holds both commercial property and equities.

www.highcroftplc.com

Land Securities
Land Securities is the biggest and best-known UK REIT and owns approximately 200 properties across the UK, focusing mainly on the London office market and large retail properties dotted around the country. The company owns some of the best-known property icons, such as Piccadilly Circus in London. In retail the focus is

mainly on out-of-town retail parks and shopping malls, such as the White Rose Shopping Centre in Leeds.

www.landsecurities.com

Liberty International

Liberty International has a property portfolio worth £7 billion made up almost entirely of prime shopping centres, including Lakeside in Thurrock, MetroCentre in Gateshead, Cribbs Causeway in Bristol, The Glades in Bromley and Braehead in Glasgow. It also owns the Covent Garden Estate in London. In total its shopping centres have 12 million sq ft of space, rented out to over 2,000 shops and attract 225 million visits from customers each year.

www.liberty-international.co.uk

Local Shopping REIT

This REIT buys local shops in urban and suburban areas throughout the UK. The portfolio consists of 627 local retail properties worth approximately £160 million.

www.localshoppingreit.co.uk

McKay Securities

The company specializes in developing and refurbishing buildings in London and the South of England, but has also completed projects elsewhere, such as in Glasgow.

www.mckaysecurities.plc.uk

Mucklow (A & J) Group

Mucklow's focus is investing in industrial and commercial properties situated close to motorway junctions and main arterial routes.

www.mucklow.com

Pineapple Corporation

This is a UK property investment company listed on the Luxembourg Stock Exchange and is one of the newest REITs. Its market capitalisation is just £18 million, making it one of the smallest companies in this sector. It has a portfolio of commercial and residential properties in the UK (mainly London) and some commercial property in Finland.

Primary Health Properties

Primary Health Properties (PHP) earns rental income from a portfolio of doctors' surgeries, pharmacies, NHS Primary Care Trusts and Health Authorities. The company owns over 100 properties worth £300 million. Approximately 85% of the space is occupied by GP surgeries.

www.phpgroup.co.uk

Rugby Estates Investment Trust

Rugby Estates is a diversified REIT. Last year it announced that it would cut jobs, sell properties and return capital to shareholders and focus more on its property management business.

www.rugbyestates.plc.uk

SEGRO - Slough Estates Group

Based in the UK, SEGRO has a listing on the London Stock Exchange and on the Euronext in Paris. SEGRO is a leading provider of flexible business space.

www.segro.com

Shaftesbury

The company invests in London's West End. The portfolio is worth over £1 billion and comprises 300 shops, 163 restaurants, 404,000 sq ft of offices and 279 apartments.

www.shaftesbury.co.uk

Town Centre Securities

The £350 million portfolio comprises mainly retail properties but also offices. Most activity is in the north of England and Scotland. The company is also an active developer with activity focused on mixed use schemes close to transport interchanges.

www.tcs-plc.com

Warner Estate Holdings

Warner Estate has a wholly owned portfolio as well as a number of joint ventures with partners. It operates a number of fund management businesses including Apia, AIF Industrial Fund, and Agora Max Shopping Centre Fund.

www.warnerestate.co.uk

Workspace Group

Workspace Group provides flexible business accommodation to small and medium sized businesses in London. The company owns over 100 properties with over 4,000 tenants generating income of over £50 million per year.

www.workspacegroup.co.uk

Chapter 8

Property Unit Trusts: Benefits & Drawbacks

There are essentially two different types of property unit trust:

- **Trusts that buy real properties**. These funds usually invest in all three types of commercial property: shops, offices and industrial, although the focus can vary considerably from fund to fund. They sometimes also hold some shares in property companies like REITs.

- **Trusts that buy property company shares**. Some property unit trusts invest only in REITs and other property company shares and do not hold any bricks-and-mortar investments. Some of these funds invest both in the UK and internationally.

Property Unit Trust Advantages

In Chapter 4 we listed the benefits of property funds over direct property investments. Most of these apply to property unit trusts:

- Income and capital gains tax free in an ISA or SIPP.

- Not stock market investments.

- No borrowings allowed.

- The investment can normally be sold in minutes.

- Big spread of properties.

- No time cost – the investment is completely passive.

- Flexibility to switch between funds without paying tax.

Although your investment will be tax free if you invest via an ISA or SIPP it is important to point out that property unit trusts do in fact pay tax on their rental income (see Property Unit Trust Disadvantages below).

The fact that property unit trusts are not quoted on any stock exchange will appeal to those who are turned off by the horrendous volatility of stock market investments.

Those in favour of REITs argue that in the long run stock exchange quoted property companies track the underlying property market. However, the fact remains that in the short run you have an investment that can rise or fall by as much as 10% in one day!

The fact that unit trusts cannot borrow money is both an advantage and a disadvantage. If what you want is to invest in a big spread of properties, without worrying about how much the fund manager has borrowed, a property unit trust may be the best solution.

Turning to the liquidity issue, although most unit trust investments can be cashed in quickly in *normal* market conditions, recent experience has shown that, in times of panic selling, property unit trusts are extremely illiquid investments.

Although low costs are a feature of many property funds, property unit trusts have high initial costs. Upfront charges of 5% or more are not uncommon, although a better deal can often be obtained if you invest through one of the ISA supermarkets (see Chapter 22).

Property Unit Trust Disadvantages

Property unit trusts also suffer from a number of drawbacks:

- They pay tax.

- They are not allowed to borrow money.

- Can be more volatile than bricks and mortar property.

- No exposure to residential property at present.

- No 'genuine bargains' available.

Once again, a few extra points are worth mentioning.

If you invest via an ISA or SIPP the income you receive from the property fund will be completely tax free. So will your capital gains when you sell the investment.

However, it is important to point out that property unit trusts do themselves pay tax. They are exempt from tax on capital gains but they pay corporation tax at 20% on their *rental* profits.

This fact is kept hidden from investors and only comes to light if you read the footnotes in their annual accounts.

So when you see fund management companies advertising "tax-efficient" property investments, remember that they are not being entirely truthful.

Because they pay tax on their rental income property unit trusts are less tax efficient than REITs (remember REITs generally pay no tax at all).

To level the playing field the Government did change the tax law in April 2008. They introduced a new type of fund called the Property Authorised Investment Fund (PAIF).

A property unit trust can convert itself into a PAIF so that it pays no tax on its rental income and enjoys the same tax benefits as its REIT cousins.

That's the good news. The bad news is that none of the existing property unit trusts have taken the plunge and converted! As a result property unit trust investors are receiving up to 20% less rental income than they should because the taxman is taking a slice.

The reason none of the property unit trusts have converted into the more tax efficient PAIF format is probably due to conversion cost considerations and a general lack of interest from investors in property funds following the poor returns of recent years.

However, it is hoped that more funds will start to convert and become more tax efficient as the property market improves. Then we will have property funds which have all the tax benefits of REITs without the requirement of a stock exchange listing.

Borrowing Restrictions

Property unit trusts are not allowed to borrow money to invest. In contrast, REITs and other property funds are allowed to boost their returns using significant amounts of gearing.

Borrowing money to invest in property can be extremely risky and many fund managers have made a complete hash of managing their borrowings, being caught with far too much debt when the market started falling in 2007.

Nevertheless when the property market does eventually recover, investors who gear up their returns using borrowed money will enjoy far higher returns than those who do not. For this reason, the restriction on property unit trusts ability to borrow at the bottom of the property cycle can be seen as a disadvantage.

Volatility

I describe property unit trusts as being "a bit" more volatile than direct property.

If a property unit trust invests only in bricks-and-mortar properties it will probably be no more volatile than any other property investment.

In practice, some property unit trusts have in the past had significant holdings of REIT shares (20% or more). This has made their prices slightly more volatile.

In recent times many of the big property unit trusts, such as Aviva Investors Property Trust and New Star UK Property have stopped investing in REITs due to their dismal returns and currently only invest in bricks and mortar.

Discounts & Premiums

Unlike REITs, property unit trusts never trade at a premium or discount. The price you pay is simply the price of the underlying properties.

Chapter 9

Directory of Property Unit Trusts

It's time to take a closer look at some of the property unit trusts on offer.

In the following pages you'll find details of several UK property unit trusts offered by some big names in the investment business.

We'll take a look at what type of property the funds have bought and in what part of the country.

Each listing also contains contact details for the fund.

All of the funds listed here focus on investing in bricks and mortar property – real buildings – rather than property shares.

Also, all of the funds concentrate on UK property – we'll take a look at global funds in Chapter 12.

More information on the funds is available from trustnet.com. There you'll also find the very latest performance figures for each of the trusts.

Please note that these are NOT recommendations to buy.

Before you invest any of your money I suggest you have a chat with a suitably qualified financial adviser (although many advised their clients to invest just before prices crashed so their value is questionable!)

Aviva Investors Property Trust

Formerly known as Norwich Property Trust this fund currently has £1.3 billion of assets. Approximately 95% is invested in 90 physical properties with the rest in cash. Offices are the biggest holding (33%), followed by retail warehousing (20%), industrial (15%), high street retail (14) and shopping centres (9%). The properties are spread fairly evenly throughout the UK.

Units in the fund have fallen from around 205p to 110p since early 2007 – a drop of 46%! At the time of writing the fund paid approximately 5% income. In an ISA that is equivalent to earning a net rental yield of 8% if you are a higher-rate taxpayer. (Note: that's an historic yield based on previous income distributions and is not guaranteed in the future.)

www.avivainvestors.co.uk/customer/our-funds/property-funds

Ignis UK Property

You may not have heard of Ignis Asset Management but the firm manages around £65 billion of assets. The property fund holds approximately 50 properties worth £388 million, spread evenly among offices, retail and industrial. One of the properties it owns is Stock Exchange House in Glasgow's prime shopping location, Buchanan St.

Units in the fund have fallen from almost 140p in 2007 to 88p – a drop of 37%. The historic yield is 5.7%.

www.ignisasset.com

L&G UK Property Trust

The total portfolio is worth £180 million divided among 40 properties but also a large 30% defensive cash holding which will be used to buy property when good deals are identified. The fund also holds a portfolio of REITs.

Units in the fund have fallen from 56p to 37p – a fall of 34%. The historic income yield is 3.6%.

www.legalandgeneral.com/investments/managers-reports

M&G Property Portfolio

The fund has around £600 million of assets, 16% of which is in cash. Fund manager Fiona Rowley is expecting to use this money shortly to snap up bargain properties. She currently favours regional offices (not London) and retail warehouses. The average lease length in the portfolio is 13 years so the fund is well cushioned against rent declines that are expected to continue for the next couple of years. The fund currently has 28% in offices, 26% in industrial, 22% in shopping centres and shops and 19% in retail warehouses. The properties are spread throughout the UK with 34% in the South East, 27% in the Midlands, 20% in Scotland, and just 8% in London.

Units in the fund have fallen from around 105p at the peak in 2007 to 65p – a fall of 38%. The fund currently has a yield of approximately 4%.

www.mandg.co.uk

New Star UK Property

The total portfolio is valued at £660 million, 87% of which is bricks and mortar property and 13% cash. The fund currently has 58 properties divided into offices (43%), retail (26%) and industrial (16%). The fund has been selling properties recently, especially those with shorter leases, to boost the average lease length of the fund (currently 10 years) and increase liquidity so that it can take advantage of new opportunities.

Units in the fund have fallen from around 160p at the peak in 2007 to 80p – a fall of 50%. The fund currently has an historic yield of 5.72%.

www.newstaram.com

Skandia Property Fund

This fund has £277 million of assets with 20 properties in the portfolio. It's biggest asset (accounting for 11% of the portfolio) is the Hulme Retail Park (Asda) in Manchester. The average vacancy rate is 6% and the average lease length is almost 11 years. The fund has a heavy retail weighting (49%) with 18% in offices and 33% in industrial property. London accounts for 20% of the portfolio with 34% in the South East and 47% in the rest of the UK.

Units in the fund have fallen from around 60p at the peak in 2007 to 34p – a fall of 43%. The historic yield is 5.2%.

www.skandiainvestmentmanagement.com

SWIP Property Trust

This fund is managed by Scottish Widows Investment Partnership (SWIP). It has £829 million of assets and up until recently 26% was kept in cash to take advantage of the downturn in property prices. Gerry Ferguson, the manager of the fund, has now started buying properties again and recently purchased three new properties in prime locations with average leases of 17 years. Around 42% of the portfolio is offices, with 37% in retail and 18% in industrial buildings.

Units in the fund have fallen from around 130p at the peak in 2007 to 80p – a fall of 38%. The historic yield is 4.1%.

www.swip.com

Threadneedle UK Property

This fund has £38 million of assets. None of its properties are in London and 77% are in the North, Yorkshire/Humberside and the Midlands.

Units in the fund have been quite resilient and fallen from around 96p at the peak in 2007 to 75p – a fall of just 21%. The fund managers put this down to property selection and a relatively high percentage in cash. The historic yield is 3.4%.

www.threadneedle.com

Chapter 10

Property Investment Companies: Benefits & Drawbacks

Investment companies are the third major type of property fund, also known as property investment trusts. These were the predecessors of REITs and, before 2006, the only way you could put property investments into an ISA.

Like REITs they're quoted on the stock market but are usually based in offshore jurisdictions such as Guernsey, where they enjoy certain tax breaks. They're managed by some of the biggest and most reputable fund management companies in the UK, including Standard Life and Scottish Widows.

You'll find these companies quoted in the *Financial Times* under 'Investment Companies'.

They have a number of benefits over property unit trusts and are an alternative to investing in REITs.

Property Investment Company Benefits

Property investment companies offer the following benefits:

- **They can borrow money**. Property investment companies use gearing to boost their returns; property unit trusts do not borrow money. Borrowing money makes the investment more risky but can also lead to higher returns.

- **Lower charges.** Upfront and annual charges of property unit trusts are often twice as high as those of investment companies.

- **Higher income yields.** For a number of reasons property investment companies tend to have higher initial yields than property unit trusts. For example, Standard Life's Property Income Trust currently pays a dividend of 4p per share. At the time of writing the shares cost 45p so that translates into an income yield of 9%. In an ISA that's completely tax free and is equivalent to earning 15% from a traditional property if you're a higher rate taxpayer.

However, what you have to be wary of is property investment companies that pay income out of the fund's capital. Many have done this in the past and it is not a sustainable practice when capital growth is weak. You should check the fund's dividend cover: make sure the fund's rental profits exceed the income payout by a significant percentage.

Property Investment Company Disadvantages

- **More volatile than unit trusts**. Property investment companies, like REITs, are listed on the stock market, which means their prices fluctuate more wildly than property unit trusts.

- **Discount and premiums**. Property investment companies, like REITs, can trade at a premium or discount to their underlying assets. If a premium turns into a discount the investor could easily lose 20% or more of his money in a very short space of time.

Chapter 11

Directory of Property Investment Companies

This chapter contains listings for some of the property investment companies on offer. Again, all of the funds listed focus on investing in bricks and mortar property rather than property shares such as REITs. Also, all of the funds concentrate on UK property – global funds are covered in Chapter 12.

More information on the funds, including the very latest performance figures, is available from trustnet.com.

F&C Commercial Property Trust

The fund has £765 million of assets. It has borrowings of £230 million but also has a large cash position of £160 million, so the total gearing is approximately 10% which is relatively modest.

Most of the properties are offices and retail (around 46% and 48% respectively), with the balance invested in industrial properties. The properties are spread throughout the UK but around 70% are in London and the South East and the rest further north.

The current share price is 75p. The fund currently pays a dividend of 6p which puts it on a yield of 8%.

www.fandc.com

ING UK Real Estate Income Trust

This fund has approximately 50 properties valued at £390 million. The fund also has £225 million of debt. If you take into account the cash it holds, net gearing is approximately 50%. The fund has recently been forced to sell property to repay debt. The properties are spread all over Britain and divided among retail (12%), offices (47%), industrial (30%), leisure (5%) and retail warehouses (7%).

The net asset value is approximately 52p per share. With the shares trading at 33p, this represents a significant discount to net asset value. The dividend is currently 4p per share which means the fund has a dividend yield of 12%. Note, however, that this income is not guaranteed and dividends have been curtailed by this fund in the past.

www.ingreit.co.uk

Invista Foundation Property

This fund has £305 million of property and a 42% loan to value ratio. The fund has sold £110 million of property since 2008 and may sell more assets. Most of the properties are offices (45%), with the balance in retail (25%) and industrial (25%). Around 60% of the portfolio is in London or the South East. There are 60 properties in the portfolio with an average value of £5 million.

The current share price is 32p and the current net asset value is 44p, so the shares trade on a discount. The fund expects to pay a dividend of 0.88p per quarter which would produce a dividend yield of 11%.

www.ifpt.co.uk

Isis Property Trust

Most of this £100 million fund's portfolio is in London and the South East (67%) and fairly evenly spread between offices (38%), industrial (29%) and retail (25%). The shares have fallen from around 160p in 2007 to 84p – approximately 50%. They were as low as 53p when the stock market reached its March 2009 lows but have since recovered and the fund's discount has all but evaporated. The projected annual dividend is 8p per share which puts the fund on a dividend yield of 10%.

www.isispropertytrust.co.uk

Standard Life Property Income Trust

This fund was discussed in detail in Chapter 2.

Chapter 12

Tax-free Overseas Property Investments

Up until recently investing in overseas property was all the rage. The UK residential and commercial property markets were expensive so investors spread their wings and looked for cheap property in Europe, the Far East, and numerous exotic locations.

Now that the UK property market has fallen so dramatically many investors are looking for bargains closer to home and interest in overseas property seems to have fizzled out.

In this chapter I'll take a brief look at the benefits and drawbacks of global property funds versus investing directly yourself.

I'll also provide details of funds that private individuals can invest in tax free through their ISAs and SIPPs.

Global Property Funds – The Benefits

Most of the benefits of property funds over direct property outlined in Chapter 4 also apply to *overseas* property funds:

- Tax-free income and capital gains.

- Your investment will normally be liquid (ie, easy to sell).

- You will own a spread of properties, not just one or two.

- You don't have to borrow any money.

- No time spent looking after properties or searching for tenants.

- No knowledge of overseas property markets required.

Property funds also offer other benefits to overseas investors:

- Less tax red tape to worry about.

- Less risk of being ripped off.

- Access to commercial property, not just residential.

- Big spread of properties across countries.

Some of these are worth discussing in a bit more detail.

Advantage #1 - Tax Savings and Red Tape

When you buy property overseas you're still subject to UK income tax on your rental profits and UK capital gains tax when you sell your property. You will probably also have to pay taxes in the country where the property is located. These taxes are usually allowed as a credit against your UK tax bill.

The end result is you will probably end up paying, at the very least, the same amount of tax as you would on a UK property. However, sometimes you will pay more. If the overseas tax takes a form that the UK authorities do not recognize (wealth tax is a good example) then no credit will be given. And if the overseas tax *exceeds* UK tax, Her Majesty's Revenue & Customs will not give you a refund.

If you invest in an overseas property fund through your ISA or SIPP you don't have to pay tax either in the UK or overseas. The fund itself may have to pay some tax but this won't affect your cash flow. If the fund invests in real estate investment trusts (REITs) then it too will probably not have any tax to worry about.

It's not just the financial drain of taxes overseas investors have to worry about – red tape can be equally painful. You'll probably have to complete some type of tax return in the other country (as well as the UK), which can be a real chore if you do not speak the local language.

Property fund investors don't have to worry about tax compliance – the fund manager will take care of any local taxes and red tape.

Advantage #2 - No Time Spent Managing Properties & Tenants

Managing an overseas property portfolio is much more time consuming than managing a UK portfolio. Tasks that are difficult to carry out long distance include finding tradesmen to carry out repairs or tenants to occupy the properties.

One solution is to use a local letting agent. In theory, that person will make sure your property is well maintained and generates a reliable rental income.

In practice, as anyone who invests in UK property knows, you can rarely rely on a letting agent to do all the graft for you. Turning an overseas property into a successful investment is likely to be much more of a struggle.

Property fund investors do not have to worry about property management issues. The investment is completely passive and looked after by a full-time professional team.

Advantage #3 - You Don't Require Overseas Property Knowledge

One of the most difficult jobs for any investor is choosing what property to buy. That's why many stick to one particular area. Over the years you acquire valuable knowledge about which streets attract tenants, what level of rent to expect and what price to pay to snap up a bargain.

When you buy overseas property you have to work a lot harder. First of all you have to pick which continent, country, and city are likely to deliver the best profits. Then you have to pick the right property. In this day and age of the internet and cheap flights a lot of research can be carried out online and by visiting the country in question. However, you're probably never going to acquire an intimate knowledge and feel for any overseas property market. It's this intimate knowledge that separates the successful investor from the lucky one.

There are lots of UK property investment companies that will hold your hand when you buy abroad. Most of them earn a commission or fee for promoting specific deals. Some of these companies do a good job; others are simply out to make a quick buck.

Most promoters of overseas property investments are nowhere near as transparent as the big fund management companies. You have no idea how good their investment recommendations are because they have no published track record. By contrast, property funds regularly have their investments independently valued and make this information available to the public.

In summary, if you want to make successful overseas property investments you either have to do a lot of research on your own or rely on someone else. That 'someone else' could be anyone ranging from an unregulated property promoter about whom you know very little to a regulated firm with an established track record.

Advantage #4 - Less Risk of Being Ripped Off

There are lots of horror stories in the press about overseas property investments that have gone horribly wrong. The worst of these involve outright loss of the investors' money because of theft, developers going bankrupt or legal cock-ups. However, for every overseas investor who experiences this sort of calamity there are thousands more being ripped off in far more subtle ways.

It all revolves around the somewhat murky world of off-plan property. In case you had any romantic notions, companies that sell overseas property do not, as a general rule, drive around the local countryside looking for 18th century stone cottages with panoramic views.

Property investment companies take a far more industrial approach to their money making. Typically, they approach developers and offer to take big blocks of new flats off their hands. These properties are usually off plan (ie, they haven't been built yet). In return the promoter receives either a kickback from the developer or a fee from the UK investor. Usually the investor is offered some sort of discount or other enticement.

Those in the property industry take it for granted that almost all of these discounts are bogus. It's not even worth dignifying the subject with any detailed discussion. Nine times out of ten if someone offers you a discount you should laugh at them.

The more subtle rip-off in the overseas property game, however, is the fact that investors are being sold poor-quality property in poor-quality locations.

It's not much better in the UK, for that matter. I like to compare new properties to new cars. Everyone knows that new cars plummet in value when you drive them out of the showroom. New properties suffer from a similar fate. In recent times prices of new apartments in the UK have fallen by over 50% in some cities. This is thanks to an oversupply caused partly by greedy developers who built on every scrap of land they could. Some of these apartment blocks are shoddily built and located in areas with inadequate infrastructure and amenities.

It's not uncommon for the majority of flats in new developments to be sold to gullible investors who all end up in what can best be described as 'buy-to-let ghettos'. Some of these properties are virtually impossible to sell ...certainly not at the inflated prices paid by the poor investors.

In the overseas property game the danger of buying a property that is difficult to rent out or sell is far greater. This is partly because of the distances involved (a lot of investors never see the properties they buy) and partly because many buyers are attracted to the high returns on offer in emerging markets.

If you buy a property in a developing country you could find yourself at the wrong end of a legal system that has less respect for property rights, arbitrary building and planning laws and is generally more tolerant of unethical business practices.

You're far less likely to get ripped of if you invest in these countries through a fund. Authorised property funds are managed by some of the most reputable financial institutions in Britain and are also tightly regulated.

The fund itself is also less likely to get ripped off when it buys property overseas because the managers are usually very experienced and have access to teams of skilled researchers and legal experts on the ground.

Advantage #5 - Commercial Property, Not Just Residential

Most people who invest overseas buy residential property only. Investing through a fund allows you to gain exposure to the commercial sector as well.

Does commercial offer better returns? Not necessarily, but anyone who is serious about property should consider investing in both.

It's not very easy for small UK investors to buy commercial property abroad because there is very little independent information and advice available. For example, it's far easier for a private investor to make a sensible investment in a holiday flat than to choose an office or industrial unit that will appeal to a local business looking to rent premises.

Advantage #6 - Big Spread of Properties Across Countries

Your risk is lower in property funds because, not only is your money divided among lots of properties, it will also usually be spread across lots of different countries.

So you could end up owning part of an office block in Paris, a slice of a shopping mall in Singapore and a chunk of an industrial estate in Eastern Europe.

Apart from the prohibitive cost of buying big commercial properties, most private investors do not have the time or skill to make successful investments all over the globe.

Big property funds often overcome this hurdle by hiring in outside expertise – local property fund managers who understand the local market and advise on the best investments.

Advantage #7 – No Mortgage Required

With credit markets around the world freezed up, many UK investors have found it difficult to obtain mortgages to buy overseas properties, especially in emerging markets.

The worst affected are those who signed up to buy properties *before* arranging mortgages.

Many have discovered that they no longer qualify (for example, because their income isn't high enough) and have had to abandon purchases, losing substantial deposits in the process.

Borrowing in the UK, for example by remortgaging your home or other UK property, is not the answer because this exposes you to currency risk.

Firstly, there is the income risk. If the pound strengthens the rental income you receive from overseas may not be enough to cover your UK mortgage interest.

Secondly, there is the capital risk. If you borrow £50,000 to buy an overseas property and the local currency drops by 20%, your property will now be worth £40,000 but you'll still owe £50,000.

When you invest in a property fund, such as a unit trust, you do not have to borrow any money and are not exposed to these risks.

Currency Risk

Having said all that, if you invest in any type of overseas property, be it a fund or directly, you will still be exposed to currency risk.

Even if property prices are rising in your country of choice you could end up losing money if the currency is dropping even faster.

For example, I remember back in 2006 the average house price in South Africa rose by around 15%. Not bad you might say but, because the rand fell by 28% against the pound, many British investors lost money during this period.

Most overseas investors turn a blind eye to currency risk except when there are headline-grabbing catastrophes such as the 1997

Asian crisis, which started in East Asia but had ripple effects around the globe.

However, a depreciating currency, like cancer, can have a very gradual effect on your wealth. For example, in 2002 the median house price in the United States was $161,800. This would have cost a British investor around £104,000.

By the end of 2006 that house had shot up in value by 37% to $222,000. However, any British investor selling up then would have received just £113,000 – a return of just 9%.

Why? Because the dollar fell gradually over the entire period. In early 2002 £1 would have cost you just $1.42. By December 2006 £1 cost $1.96, which made bringing money back into the UK extremely expensive.

Global Property Funds – The Drawbacks

So property funds are the best way to invest overseas, is that correct? Well, not necessarily.

While outlining the drawbacks of bricks-and-mortar investment I have been playing Devil's advocate. There has been no shortage of snake oil salesmen saying how easy it is to make a fortune buying property in exotic locations, so a few words of caution can hardly go astray!

A very strong case can also be made for investing directly instead of through a fund. Apart from all the drawbacks of funds listed in Chapter 5, a few additional ones are worth mentioning:

Drawback #1 - Less Fun!

A lot of people who buy property abroad do so not just to make lots of money but because they also want a home in their favourite holiday destination.

The property may be rented out for part of the year and used by the owner at other times. Or, if affordability is not an issue, the property may be kept for the exclusive use of the owner's family and friends.

In my opinion this is one of the best ways to make successful overseas investments. If you come across a well-built attractive property in a beautiful location and you can't bear the thought of someone else snapping it up before you do, and you know your family will enjoy holidaying there for years to come, then you can be pretty sure that others will think the same and want to buy it from you one day. In other words, it will be a good investment.

This is especially true if the property has something unique about it. In other words, if it's not one of hundreds of faceless new apartments in an area where there is going to be a lot more construction work in the years ahead.

It's hard for an amateur investor to be as confident about foreign buy-to-let properties that are rented out mainly to locals. How do you really know whether that apartment on the outskirts of Warsaw or Bucharest is going to appeal to someone else if it doesn't appeal to you personally?

As for property funds there is, of course, no opportunity to enjoy your property and make lots of money at the same time. Owning part of an Eastern European industrial estate may be profitable but you're hardly going to want to take the kids there!

Drawback #2 - Less Profitable

Property funds are less risky because your money is spread among lots of property in lots of countries. However, this also makes them a lot more pedestrian than other overseas investments.

For many, the most exciting place to invest is in the emerging markets: Eastern European countries such as Poland and Romania, and exotic destinations such as Morocco, Turkey and Thailand. Investing may be more risky but investors are hoping for massive capital gains.

Property funds also invest in emerging markets – but only a portion of their money. The bulk of their funds is invested in developed economies such as Western European countries.

Very few would dare to take the big single-country bets that private investors do.

If you're confident of your property investment skills then you could make far more money going it alone and looking for your own bargains.

Directory of Global Property Funds

If you want to put your money in a global property fund you have two choices:

- Funds that buy property shares

- Funds that buy bricks-and-mortar properties

At present most global property funds invest in shares only (REITs and other property companies). However, in this section we're going to focus on the select few that invest in bricks and mortar (real property) only. That's what most private investors are interested in.

All of the funds listed in this section qualify for inclusion in both ISAs and SIPPs. I am the first to admit that the choice at present is somewhat paltry!

New Star International Property

This £330 million fund was the first international bricks and mortar commercial property unit trust. The fund currently pays income of approximately 4.6% per year – tax free in an ISA or SIPP. The minimum lump sum investment is £1,000.

The fund owns properties in Japan, Singapore, Australia, France, the Czech Republic, Germany, Poland and the Netherlands.

Unfortunately the fund has been hit hard by investor redemptions and at the time of writing was still having to sell properties to raise cash and resume dealing.

www.hendersonnewstar.com

AXA Property Trust

This is not a unit trust, it's a quoted property fund. This means it's subject to stock market volatility and can borrow money.

The focus is European Property and a significant percentage is invested in German retail properties. The fund also owns properties in the Netherlands and Italy.

The fund is currently paying income of 4p per share and the shares currently cost around 41p, so that puts it on an income yield of almost 10%.

At the time of writing the fund was trading on a very large discount to its net asset value of over 50%. However, this does not mean the shares are cheap and may reflect investors worries that a significant amount of the equity in the portfolio could be wiped out if property prices continue to fall.

The portfolio was valued at £168 million at the end of March 2009 and the fund had debt of around £80 million.

www.axa-im.co.uk

Alpha Pyrenees Trust

This is another stock market quoted fund which owns a portfolio of office and warehouse properties on the outskirts of Paris (accounting for over 80% of the portfolio). These properties are rented out to blue chip tenants such as Credit Lyonnais with rents linked to the construction price index. The rest of the portfolio consists of retail properties in Spain.

www.alphapyreneestrust.com

Kenmore European Industrial Fund

This fund is listed on the London Stock Exchange and owns industrial properties across central Europe and Scandinavia.

The shares have fallen from around 120p at their peak to 20p at the time of writing. The latest net asset value was 89p per share.

The fund has been offloading properties this year to reduce its debt and prevent its gearing ratio going to high (currently it stands at 62%).

www.kenmoreeifund.com

Part 3

Retire Rich with a Property Pension

Chapter 13

The Amazing Pension Tax Reliefs

Let's get straight down to business.

There's only one reason why you should invest your money in a pension and that is to SAVE TAX.

In this chapter I'll be taking a close look at how the pension tax reliefs operate and *exactly* how much they are worth to you at the end of the day.

To do this we'll follow the progress of two investors over many years, one investing inside a pension, the other investing outside a pension.

When you contribute to a pension plan you benefit from two important tax breaks:

- Tax relief on your contributions – what I call buying property at a 40% discount.

- Tax-free investment returns – all your rental income and capital gains will be completely tax free.

Pensions truly are fantastic tax shelters. Most of us have heard something about their tax benefits but nobody has taken a *really* close look at just how powerful these tax concessions can be.

So that's what I decided to do. Using my training as an economist, and armed with a whole bunch of spreadsheets, I decided to find out exactly how much better off you are investing through a pension compared with alternative investment routes.

I wanted to find out precisely how much more wealth you are likely to accumulate and how much more income you are likely to earn, if any, by investing through a pension plan.

The results make fascinating reading. Far from being 'boring', pensions are one of the most powerful weapons in your financial armoury.

After all, what could be more enticing than free cash? That's exactly what pensions offer you – the taxman's money and lots of it. The generous tax reliefs could allow you to earn almost 140% more income than someone who decides to invest outside a pension.

The Two Pension Tax Breaks

So what are these tax reliefs, how do they work and how much are they really worth? That's what you'll find out in this chapter. What I won't get into here are all the nitty-gritty rules, such as how much you can contribute each year.

That's important information but we'll leave it for later. It gets in the way of the really important issue, which is whether you should invest in a pension in the first place!

Let's examine each of the pension tax reliefs in turn.

Tax Relief #1 – Your Contributions

When you make pension contributions the taxman will top up your savings by paying cash directly into your plan. Effectively for every £80 you invest, the taxman will put in an extra £20.

Why £20, you might be asking? Well your contributions are treated as having been paid out of income that has already been taxed at the basic income tax rate of 20%. The taxman is therefore refunding the income tax you've already paid.

The company that manages your pension plan – usually an insurance company or 'SIPP provider' – will claim this money for you from the taxman.

So whatever contribution you make personally, divide it by 0.80 and you'll get the TOTAL amount that is invested in your plan.

Example 1

Dave invests £4,000 per year in a self-invested personal pension (SIPP). The total amount that will be invested, after the taxman makes his top-up payment, is:

$$£4,000/0.80 = £5,000$$

Basic-rate tax relief isn't the end of the story. If Dave is a *higher-rate* taxpayer, paying tax at 40%, he'll be able to claim even more tax relief.

The Cherry on Top – Higher Rate Relief

If you're a higher-rate taxpayer the taxman will let you claim the extra 20% (40% minus the 20% he's already given you) when you submit your tax return.

What's great about this tax relief is the money is not paid into your pension plan where it would be out of reach until you retire. Instead you'll get a nice cheque in the post from Her Majesty's Revenue and Customs (or a BACS transfer as is more likely the case nowadays). If you haven't paid your taxes yet, your tax bill will be reduced accordingly.

Example 2

As we already know, Dave's personal contribution is £4,000 and total pension fund investment, including the taxman's contribution, is:

$$£4,000/0.80 = £5,000$$

The £4,000 is what's known as his 'net contribution' and the £5,000 is what's known as his 'gross contribution'. Multiplying his gross contribution by 20% (40% – 20%) we get:

$$£5,000 \times 20\% = £1,000$$

This is the amount of tax that will be refunded to Dave.

Effectively he has a pension investment of £5,000, which has cost him just £3,000 (£4,000 personal contribution less his £1,000 tax refund). In other words, he is getting all his investments at a 40% discount.

This is the critical number. Being able to make investments year after year at a 40% discount can have a massive effect on the amount of wealth you can accumulate.

Summary

- When you make pension contributions you qualify for two different types of tax relief: Basic-rate tax relief which comes in the shape of top-ups to your pension plan and higher-rate relief which takes the shape of a tax refund paid to you personally.

- Your total pension fund investment is found by dividing your personal contribution by 0.80. The excess is paid by the taxman to your pension provider.

- Higher-rate relief is calculated by multiplying your gross pension fund contribution by 20%.

- Together these two tax reliefs mean all your pension investments come in at a 40% discount.

- Although basic-rate relief is paid directly into your pension fund and is out of reach until you arrive at the minimum retirement age, it's important to stress that the money is yours to invest as you please. Most personal pension plans these days, especially SIPPs, give you enormous investment flexibility.

- With higher-rate relief you don't have to use the tax refund to make other investments, although this would be the sensible thing to do. You can do whatever you like with it: go on holiday, pay off some of your mortgage or buy a new car.

Tax Break #2 – Tax-free Investment Returns

Apart from obtaining tax relief on your contributions, all your pension savings grow completely free from income tax and capital gains tax.

To see just how important this tax break is, let's take a look at an example. For now we'll ignore the fact that pension contributions also qualify for up-front tax relief and focus solely on the tax-free investment growth.

Example 1

Kwame invests £5,000 per year in a SIPP and enjoys tax-free investment growth of 7% per year. He increases the amount he invests by 3% per year to keep up with inflation.

Katrina also invests £5,000 per year in an investment that grows by 7% per year but she pays 40% tax on her returns.

How do Kwame and Katrina's returns compare? They're both contributing exactly the same amount and earning identical pre-tax returns. *So any difference is down to tax treatment alone.*

The results are summarised in Table 1. At the end of year one Kwame has his £5,000 investment plus a tax-free return of 7%, which comes to £5,350 in total. Katrina has her £5,000 investment plus an after-tax return of just 4.2%. So she is left with just £5,210 at the end of the year.

At the end of year two Kwame has his £5,350 from last year *plus* tax-free growth on that money, plus this year's investment *plus* tax-free growth on that money. In total he now has £11,235 compared with Katrina's £10,795.

And so it goes on, year after year, with Kwame enjoying tax-free growth and Katrina paying 40% of her returns to the taxman. Eventually after 10 years Kwame has £11,702 more than Katrina, after 20 years he has £71,578 more and after 30 years he has an incredible £255,607 more!

Table 1
Taxed vs Tax-Free Investment Growth

End Year	Kwame	Katrina	% Diff
1	5,350	5,210	3
2	11,235	10,795	4
3	17,697	16,776	5
4	24,782	23,173	7
5	32,538	30,011	8
6	41,018	37,311	10
7	50,278	45,099	11
8	60,377	53,401	13
9	71,381	62,244	15
10	83,358	71,656	16
11	96,383	81,667	18
12	110,535	92,309	20
13	125,900	103,614	22
14	142,570	115,617	23
15	160,642	128,353	25
16	180,222	141,861	27
17	201,423	156,180	29
18	224,366	171,351	31
19	249,179	187,417	33
20	276,003	204,425	35
21	304,986	222,420	37
22	336,287	241,454	39
23	370,079	261,578	41
24	406,543	282,847	44
25	445,876	305,317	46
26	488,289	329,049	48
27	534,007	354,105	51
28	583,272	380,550	53
29	636,341	408,453	56
30	693,493	437,886	58

The fourth column in the table shows us how much better off Kwame is proportionately. After the first couple of years the difference is very small and Kwame has just 4% more money than Katrina. But the difference grows year after year until after 30 years Kwame is left with an impressive 58% more money than Katrina and all thanks to his decision to invest in a pension scheme.

The reason Kwame becomes proportionately more wealthy with every year that passes is thanks to the 'magic' of compound interest. Every year he earns more money on every pound of his savings and reinvests those extra profits. Those extra profits in turn generate tax-free profits that are reinvested... and so on.

Compound interest is a great friend of pension savers, especially those with an eye to the long term.

Summary

- Pensions offer tax-free investment returns. This is potentially an extremely valuable tax break and could be worth tens of thousands of pounds to you over the long term.

- After 10 years you could have 16% more money than someone who pays tax on their profits, after 20 years you could have 35% more money and after 30 years you could have 58% more money.

- The longer you save, the more you will benefit from this tax break.

Putting the Two Tax Reliefs Together

So far we've seen that by contributing to a pension you can enjoy a 40% discount on your investments. We've also seen that once your money is inside a pension plan it can grow tax free.

Both of these pension tax breaks are clearly attractive in their own right. But what happens when you put them together?

Well then you have a truly powerful cocktail!

The tax savings are so large one wonders why more people don't exploit pensions to the max. It could be the difference between a very ordinary and a very prosperous retirement.

What we'll do in this section is track two investors, Donald and Warren, over the next 30 years, each of them making identical investments and earning identical returns. The only difference is Donald will invest in a pension; Warren will invest outside a pension.

You will see that after just 10 years Donald, the pension investor, will have accumulated almost twice as much money as Warren. And after 30 years Donald will be in a completely different league. His savings will have grown to £693,493, whereas Warren will have just £262,732.

Let's take a closer look at how this amazing result is obtained.

Example - Donald and Warren

At the beginning of the year Donald invests £4,000 in his personal pension plan. The taxman adds another £1,000 bringing his total investment to £5,000. Donald is a successful property developer and is a higher-rate taxpayer. As a result he claims an extra £1,000 per year in tax relief. So he has acquired £5,000 of investments for just £3,000. He increases his pension contribution by 3% per year and the money in the pension plan grows by 7% per year.

Donald's friend Warren works in the City and is also a higher-rate taxpayer. He's a bit sceptical about pensions and decides not to use one. We'll assume Warren invests £3,000 per year (which is exactly how much Donald invests out of his own pocket).

Warren also earns 7% per year but, because he pays tax at 40%, earns only 4.2% per year on his investments.

The two scenarios are summarised in Table 2.

At the end of year one Donald has pension savings of £5,000 plus tax-free growth at 7%, which comes to £5,350. Warren, on the other hand has savings of £3,000 and investment growth of 4.2%, which comes to £3,126. Already after just one year Donald has 71% more money than Warren!

At the end of year two Donald has earned another 7% on the £5,350 from last year, which comes to £5,724.50. Plus he's made a fresh contribution of £5,150 and earned 7% on that which comes to £5,510.50. In total his savings are now worth £11,235.

And what about the hapless Warren? At the end of year two he has earned another 4.2% on the £3,126 from last year and has made a fresh contribution of £3,090 and earned 4.2% on that. In total his savings are worth £6,477.

And so the process continues with Donald becoming proportionately richer than Warren with every year that passes. After 10 years he has 94% more money than Warren, after 20 years he has 125% more money and after 30 years he has 164% more money.

Donald is becoming richer because every year he is investing more than Warren and every year he is earning higher after-tax returns. These higher returns are themselves reinvested tax free to produce even higher returns the following year.

Table 2
Taxed vs Tax-Free Investment Growth

End year	Pension	No Pension	% Diff
1	5,350	3,126	71%
2	11,235	6,477	73%
3	17,697	10,065	76%
4	24,782	13,904	78%
5	32,538	18,006	81%
6	41,018	22,387	83%
7	50,278	27,059	86%
8	60,377	32,040	88%
9	71,381	37,346	91%
10	83,358	42,993	94%
11	96,383	49,000	97%
12	110,535	55,385	100%
13	125,900	62,168	103%
14	142,570	69,370	106%
15	160,642	77,012	109%
16	180,222	85,117	112%
17	201,423	93,708	115%
18	224,366	102,810	118%
19	249,179	112,450	122%
20	276,003	122,655	125%
21	304,986	133,452	129%
22	336,287	144,872	132%
23	370,079	156,947	136%
24	406,543	169,708	140%
25	445,876	183,190	143%
26	488,289	197,429	147%
27	534,007	212,463	151%
28	583,272	228,330	155%
29	636,341	245,072	160%
30	693,493	262,732	164%

Extracting Money from Your Pension

It's now time for Donald and Warren to start benefiting from all this money they've been accumulating over the years.

When you cash in your pension savings you can take 25% as a tax-free lump sum. The rest is used to fund a monthly pension that is fully taxed. This pension usually comes in the form of an annuity from a life insurance company, although there are other options which we'll examine in Chapter 14.

Although there has been tax relief on everything so far (contributions, investment growth and your lump sum), the pension is *fully taxed*. And there's a massive difference between the tax treatment of pension income and virtually every other form of investment income.

The difference is that you are taxed on both your interest AND your capital. For example, when you hand over your pension savings to buy an annuity, the life insurance company invests it in low-risk Government bonds and pays you a monthly income. The income consists of the interest on the bonds *plus* a little bit of your original capital.

By paying you back some of your capital each month your income will be higher than that available from most other investments that only pay interest. This is one of the major benefits of annuities.

What's more, the payments are guaranteed to continue for life, whether you live for another three years or another 100 years! You don't have to worry about running out of savings.

While receiving capital repayments each month is a good way of boosting your retirement income, having to pay tax on them is a distinct disadvantage. That's equivalent to putting £100 in a bank deposit and paying £40 in tax when you withdraw the money a year later.

Of course this is not what happens to your bank savings in practice. You only pay tax on the *interest* you earn and your capital will be paid back in full with no further tax liability.

So while there are tremendous tax benefits to investing in pension plans there is also a major tax penalty at the end.

The critical question is, do the upfront tax benefits – tax relief on contributions, tax-free investment growth and a tax-free lump sum – outweigh the penalty of the fully taxed pension income at the end?

This is the all-important question and I'm going to answer it shortly. However, to do that it's first important to explain why annuities are so important in pension planning, how they work in practice and the difference between pension and purchased annuities.

Are Annuities Evil?

What most people don't like about annuities is that when you die they die. Your heirs generally get nothing. However, there is a misconception among the investing public that if you die early your surplus annuity capital goes into the life insurance company's coffers.

This is actually not the case. The money is used to pay the pensions of those who live longer and who end up getting significantly more income than they originally paid in.

This is the key benefit of annuities. They protect you against one of the greatest uncertainties of all: how long you will live. They do this by redistributing income from those who die younger to those who die older.

The amount of annuity income you get will depend on a variety of factors. The most important ones are your age (the older you are the higher the income), your sex (women live longer so get less income each month) and the current level of interest rates (the insurer will invest your money in Government bonds that earn interest so the higher the level of interest rates the higher your annuity income).

Pension vs Purchased Annuities

There are essentially two types of annuity:

- Pension annuities – the type of annuity you buy with your pension plan savings.

- Purchased annuities – the type of annuity anyone with a lump sum can buy.

There are two major differences between the two types of annuity:

- Purchased annuities pay less income than pension annuities because the market for them is less competitive and because people who volunteer to buy them generally live longer than average.

- With purchased annuities the capital portion of the payment is *completely tax free*. As a result, the after-tax income is often much higher than other investments.

Annuity rates vary significantly from insurer to insurer, depending on how eager these companies are to attract your business. The Financial Services Authority (FSA) produces a useful comparison of annuity quotes from different insurance companies on its website: www.fsa.gov.uk/tables.

A sample quote from one big insurer is contained in Table 3.

As you can see, the pension annuity income is quite a bit higher than the purchased annuity income. However, most of the purchased annuity income comes in the form of capital repayment and is therefore completely tax free.

Back now to Donald and Warren to see who ends up better off in retirement.

Table 3
Annual Annuity Rates

Male age 65 with £100,000
Annual income, no inflation protection

Pension annuity	**£7,280.40**
Purchased Annuity	**£6,819.96**

Of which:

Tax-free capital portion	£5,671
Taxable interest portion	£1,148.96

Donald and Warren – The Final Outcome

Just to recap, in the previous example Donald (investing in a pension) and Warren (not using a pension) ended up with the following savings after different time periods.

	Donald £	Warren £
After 5 years	32,538	18,006
After 10 years	83,358	42,993
After 15 years	160,642	77,012
After 20 years	276,003	122,655
After 25 years	445,876	183,190
After 30 years	693,493	262,732

We know that Donald has significantly higher pension savings than Warren but what happens when both investors start using their savings to produce income. How much better off is Donald then?

This is the million-dollar question because the only reason to invest in a SIPP or other pension scheme is to generate a secure income when you retire.

So the true benefit of investing in pensions will only be revealed when we compare Donald's final income with Warren's final income. However, to make sure we're comparing apples with apples it's essential to assume that both investors put their money into identical income-producing investments.

Donald can take 25% of his pension savings as a tax-free lump sum and do what he wants with the money. The remaining 75% eventually has to be used to produce a regular pension income. Although Donald has some flexibility here (see Chapter 14), we'll assume he opts for a pension annuity. In practice this is the choice most pension investors who need a high and secure income will make.

Warren, who didn't invest through a pension, can do what he likes with all of his money. However, if we assume that he invests in, say, rental property, bank deposits or shares, we will not be comparing apples with apples.

It's impossible to compare Donald's annuity with any other form of investment income. Annuities are completely risk free because they pay you a guaranteed income for life. Shares, property and other investments cannot make this promise.

So to ensure that Donald and Warren are investing in comparable income-producing assets we have to assume that Warren also buys an annuity with all of his savings. Because he hasn't been investing in a pension, Warren will buy a purchased annuity.

In summary we assume that Donald and Warren take their savings and do the following:

- Donald uses 75% of his savings to buy a pension annuity for life.

- Donald uses his 25% tax-free lump sum to buy a purchased annuity for life.

- Warren uses all his savings to buy a purchased annuity for life.

I'll use the annuity quotes from Table 3 and assume both Donald and Warren are 65 when they decide to retire. The final income calculation is contained in Table 4.

Table 4
Final Income Comparison

Donald's Income Calculation After 30 Years

Pension Annuity:

	£
Total pension savings	693,493
75% Pension Annuity Purchase	520,120
Annual Annuity @ £7,280.40 per £100,000	37,867
Less tax @ 20%	**30,294**

Purchased Annuity

Lump sum - 25% of £693,493	173,373
Annual Annuity @ £6,819.96 per £100,000	11,824

Of which:

Tax-free capital portion	9,832
Taxable interest portion	1,992
Less tax @ 20%	398
Total Purchased Annuity Income	**11,426**

Total Pension Income	**41,720**

Warren's Income Calculation After 30 Years

Purchased Annuity

Total savings	262,732
Annual Annuity @ £6,819.96 per £100,000	17,918

Of which:

Tax-free capital portion	14,900
Taxable interest portion	3,019
Less tax @ 20%	604

Total Purchased Annuity Income	**17,315**

Note: Assumption is Donald and Warren are basic-rate taxpayers when they retire and pay tax at 20% on their pensions.

At the end of the day Donald ends up with income of £41,720 compared with Warren's £17,315.

Put another away, Donald has two and a half times as much income as Warren. This result is staggering and shows the true power of the pension tax break. Remember Donald and Warren made *identical investments* each year and earned *identical pre-tax returns*.

The only difference is Donald put his money in a pension plan while Warren invested outside a pension.

I've assumed both end up as basic-rate taxpayers and do not pay tax at 40% – most people end up in this situation when they retire.

Shorter Savings Periods

The above example showed final income after 30 years. This may sound like a long time but it's not really. That's equivalent to starting investing at the age of 35, which is not an unreasonable age to start contributing to a pension plan. Many investors start contributing earlier.

However, for those with a shorter time horizon it's important to show how the pension vs non-pension results compare if we assume savings take place for a much shorter period of time. For example, if you're 50 years old now you've only got another 15 years to make pension contributions, if you want to retire at 65. Is the pension route still as profitable?

Table 5 shows the final retirement incomes of Donald, the pension plan saver, and Warren, the non-pension saver, over a range of time periods. In this table we're assuming that there are lots of Donalds and Warrens of different ages! One pair reaches age 65 after saving for five years, one pair reaches age 65 after saving for 10 years and the final pair reaches age 65 after saving for 30 years.

Income is calculated in exactly the same way as in Table 4.

Table 5
Retirement Income over Different Time Periods

	Donald	Warren	% Difference
After 5 years	1,957	1,187	65
After 10 years	5,015	2,833	77
After 15 years	9,664	5,075	90
After 20 years	16,604	8,083	105
After 25 years	26,823	12,073	122
After 30 years	41,720	17,315	141

The results speak for themselves. The shorter the time period the smaller the gap between the two savers. However, even over short time periods Donald, the pension saver, still ends up with a lot more income than Warren. Even after contributing to a pension for just five years Donald still ends up with 65% more income.

Basic-rate Taxpayers

So far we've shown how a *higher-rate* taxpayer can earn a much higher retirement income by contributing to a pension plan. Higher-rate taxpayers are those earning over £43,875 this year.

What about those who earn less. Are pensions still attractive to basic-rate taxpayers?

The only way to find out is by following another two investors over the course of their working lives. We'll use exactly the same methods as before so we can fast track the process and get straight to the results.

Example

David and Michael are great footballers. Although they had dreams of making it big they never quite managed to pull it off. Both now teach PE at the local comprehensive.

Table 6
Pension vs Non-pension Returns
Basic-rate Taxpayers

	Pension	No Pension	% Diff
After 5 years	1,468	1,236	19
After 10 years	3,761	3,055	23
After 15 years	7,248	5,673	28
After 20 years	12,452	9,375	33
After 25 years	20,116	14,542	38
After 30 years	31,288	21,684	44

They're both quite frugal with their spending and decide to start saving £3,000 per year for retirement. David has a razor-sharp mind for figures and decides to save through a pension. Michael, on the other hand, decides to save outside a pension. David's total pension investment in year one will be £3,750 after the taxman has topped it up (£3,000/0.80). Michael's total investment will be just £3,000.

Again we assume that both of them earn 7% per year, which means Michael will earn just 5.6% after paying tax at 20%. They also increase their contributions by 3% per year.

And how do they fare when they start drawing income at age 65? As before we'll assume that David uses 75% of his pension savings to buy a pension annuity and takes the rest as a tax-free lump sum and uses it to buy a purchased annuity. Michael uses all his savings to buy a purchased annuity.

The after-tax incomes they both receive are summarised in Table 6.

Once again the results speak loud and clear. No matter how long David invests he earns significantly more income than Michael. Even after just five years David is almost 20% better off.

Clearly basic-rate taxpayers should also consider saving through a pension.

However, basic-rate taxpayers who expect to become higher-rate taxpayers in the future, should also consider deferring contributions until then so as to maximize their tax savings.

National Insurance Savings

So far we've illustrated how much *income tax* you can save by contributing to a pension plan.

But what about the other tax that decimates your pay cheque each month? The tax I am referring to, of course, is national insurance. It has become one of the Government's favourite revenue spinners in recent years.

National insurance is calculated as follows for the current 2009/10 tax year:

- Employees pay no national insurance on the first £5,715 of earnings. They then pay 11% on earnings between £5,715 and £43,875 and 1% on earnings over £43,875.

- Employers pay 12.8% national insurance on every single pound the employee earns over the £5,715 earnings threshold. There is no cap.

From April 6th 2010 all of the above tax rates will increase by 0.5%.

One relatively easy – and perfectly legal – way to avoid national insurance and increase your pension pot is to get your employer to contribute directly into your pension fund, instead of paying the contributions yourself.

This can be achieved through something called *salary sacrifice*. Here's how it works:

- The employee agrees to take a pay cut.

- The employer agrees to pay that money into the employee's pension fund.

- There is no national insurance on employer pension contributions, so the employee saves up to 11% of the salary sacrifice amount and the employer saves up to 12.8%.

- Most employers agree to share the 12.8% saving with the employee by increasing the pension contribution (they are not legally obliged too, however).

106

Many small employers do not have a company pension scheme. However, salary sacrifice works even if the contributions are paid into a SIPP or any other personal pension or stakeholder plan, giving the employee complete control over how the money is invested.

More Pay & More Pension

With salary sacrifice it is possible to have the best of both worlds: a higher income AND higher pension contributions at no extra cost to your employer. The only person who loses out is the taxman!

Example – Before Salary Sacrifice

Jake earns £30,000 and pays £1,200 into his SIPP. The taxman tops this up with £300, bringing his total pension contribution to £1,500.

His income tax bill is £4,705 and his national insurance bill is £2,671.

In summary his disposable income is £21,424 and he has £1,500 of pension savings.

Example – After Salary Sacrifice

Jake now agrees to sacrifice £1,500 of salary and in return his employer agrees to contribute £1,500 to Jake's SIPP.

Jake's salary has been reduced so:

- *His income tax bill falls from £4,705 to £4,405.*
- *His national insurance falls from £2,671 to £2,506.*

Jake's disposable income increases by £165 to £21,589.

Jake's employer saves £192 national insurance (£1,500 x 12.8%) and agrees to add this to the pension contribution, bringing the total contribution to £1,692.

In summary, Jake's disposable income increases by £165 to £21,589 and his pension contributions increase by £192 to £1,692. In total he is £357 better off.

In the above example the total pension contribution was relatively modest. Even bigger national insurance savings can be achieved by upping the contributions.

Those employees earning more than £43,875 will only save 1% national insurance from salary sacrifice, rising to 1.5% from next year. So for this group it is imperative that the employer agrees to pass on some or all of the 12.8% saving.

Implementing Salary Sacrifice

It's important to point out that salary sacrifice must be a contractual agreement, not an informal arrangement between you and your employer.

However, your contract of employment can be altered by using a simple agreement letter and many pension companies provide sample documentation.

It's also important that your terms of employment are changed *before* the salary sacrifice commences and the sacrificed amount must appear on your payslip as a salary reduction and not as an entry under "deductions".

HM Revenue Customs is not against salary sacrifice but could challenge the arrangement if it has not been set up correctly and the paperwork is not in order.

HMRC will not allow salary sacrifice if you can at any time revert to your original pay package.

According to Scottish Life a contract alteration will usually last for 12 months so that it fits in with salary reviews: "The salary exchange agreement should state that the variation is time bounded and that the original contract will be reinstated at the end of the salary exchange period. A new agreement should therefore be arranged at the end of each agreement period if the salary exchange is to continue."

Potential Drawbacks

Salary sacrifice arrangements have some potential drawbacks. Some of these are relatively easy to mitigate but others are unavoidable and could reduce the potential savings:

- Any salary reduction could affect the amount of money you can borrow, for example to buy a house. One way around this would be to get your employer to provide the lender with a letter of reference confirming the total pay package to which you are entitled. It is possible that some lenders will not accept this, however.

- Reducing your salary could reduce some of your employment benefits (eg overtime and future pay increases). Many salary sacrifice arrangements deal with this by basing any benefits on the original salary – also known as the reference salary or notional salary. So if you are currently earning £40,000 and reduce your salary to £37,000, your benefits should be calculated as if you are earning £40,000.

- Salary sacrifice could affect your entitlement to certain salary-linked state benefits such as the state second pension. Salary sacrifice will not affect your basic state pension, however. The basic state pension is not based on the amount of national insurance you pay. As long as you have a full national insurance history you will receive the full amount when you reach the state pension age.

- Maternity pay is usually calculated as a percentage of earnings so could be impacted by salary sacrifice.

- On the plus side a reduction in your salary could increase your working tax credit entitlement.

Summary

- In this chapter we've tried to work out exactly how valuable the pension tax breaks are.

- Pension plans offer two major tax breaks: tax relief on contributions and tax-free investment growth.

- Tax relief on contributions means you receive a discount of up to 40% on your investments.

- When you contribute £100 the taxman will top this up and your total investment will be £125 (£100/0.80).

- You may also receive higher-rate relief: 20% x £125 = £25.

- When you retire, 25% can be taken as a tax-free lump sum.

- The remaining 75% is used to produce pension income.

- When comparing pension and non-pension investing you have to compare apples with apples. In our examples we assume both investors use their money to buy annuities.

- There are two different types of annuity: pension and purchased. Pension annuities pay a higher income but are fully taxed. Purchased annuities are mostly tax free.

- In our examples we showed that a higher-rate taxpayer could earn 140% more retirement income than someone who invests outside a pension plan. Even after just five years the pension saver ends up with 65% more income.

- Basic-rate taxpayers also score heavily by investing through a pension. After five years you could end up with almost 20% more income and after 30 years you could be 44% better off.

- Significant national insurance savings can be enjoyed if your employer agrees to a salary sacrifice arrangement.

Chapter 14

Plain-English Guide to the New Pension Rules

On April 6th 2006 – also known as A-Day – a new set of rules was introduced that governs every aspect of pension investing.

In this chapter I will attempt to translate the most important and interesting of these new rules into plain English and show you how to use them to your advantage.

Then in Chapter 15 we'll take a closer look at the specific changes affecting property investors, in particular what *types* of property you can put in your pension.

It's important to note that some of these rules could change over time. The Government has already tampered with some of the most exciting changes, including the rule that allowed direct residential property investment and the rule that allowed pension savings to be passed to heirs.

Tax Relief on Contributions

Tax relief on contributions is the most important tax break offered by pension plans because it allows you to buy property and other assets at a 40% discount.

Up until a few years ago the contribution limits were quite stingy. For example, members of occupational pension schemes could only contribute up to 15% of their earnings and members of personal pension schemes could only contribute between 17.5% and 40%, depending on their age.

For most people these limits were more than adequate. Very few of us put away as much as 15% of our salaries, let alone 40%. However, there are times when being able to make large one-off pension contributions is extremely useful, for example if you earn a large bonus or have a large lump sum to invest.

Another problem with the old pension rules was that members of occupational pension schemes could not belong to a second pension scheme. As a result many employees could not set up their own self-invested personal pensions (SIPPs) and this placed enormous restrictions on their retirement planning.

Generally you have no control over how your employer's pension fund invests your retirement savings. For example, if you are very young you may want to invest most of your pension savings in stock market investments or property rather than government bonds or other low-growth investments.

Alternatively, if you're a knowledgeable property investor you may want to invest *all* of your retirement capital in property. No company pension scheme will let you do this.

Since April 6th 2006 the restrictive contribution limits and membership rules have been be scrapped.

Most people can now contribute as much as they like to as many pension plans as they like and decide for themselves how their savings are invested.

For the current 2009/10 tax year the annual allowance is the *lower* of:

- Your entire annual earnings or
- £245,000

So if you earn, say, £60,000 in salary or business profits you'll be able to make pension contributions of £60,000 and effectively pay no income tax on your earnings.

The annual allowance has been set at £255,000 for each of the years 2010/11 to 2015/16.

It's important to note that the above contribution limits are for 'gross contributions', not net cash contributions. Your gross contribution *includes* the taxman's top up and is found by dividing the amount you personally contribute by 0.80.

Other important points to note about the new contribution limit are the following:

- 'Earnings' do not include investment income (for example, rental income and dividends). In other words, if you're earning lots of rental income it will *not* be treated as earnings when it comes to making pension contributions.

- Everyone can make a minimum contribution of £3,600 per year.

- If your contributions exceed the maximum allowed a charge of 40% will be levied.

- Both an employer and employee's contributions count towards the annual allowance. In other words, the contributions of both you and your employer must not exceed £245,000 in the 2009/2010 tax year.

Pension Contributions in Practice

While most people contribute just a small percentage of their earnings to their pension schemes, the new '100% of earnings' rule is extremely attractive to those earning windfall profits, bonuses and other large but irregular lump sums.

It is now possible to invest these amounts (which are usually taxed at 40%) in a SIPP and obtain full tax relief.

Making large one-off pension contributions is not always a good strategy, however. Even if you're a higher-rate taxpayer you only get higher-rate tax relief **to the extent that you have earnings taxed at 40%**.

So if only £5,000 of your earnings is taxed at 40%, you will only receive higher-rate tax relief on £5,000... even if you make a £20,000 pension contribution.

You'll always receive full basic-rate tax relief (the 20% contributed by the taxman) but you might only receive the *extra* 20% higher-rate relief on a small portion of your contribution.

To enjoy the maximum tax relief – and ensure that you really are getting your investments at a 40% discount – you may have to spread your contributions over a number of tax years.

Example 1

Sandy earns a salary of £60,000 in the 2009/2010 tax year. For now we'll assume he makes no pension contributions. His total tax bill is calculated as follows:

	£
Earnings	*60,000*
Less: personal allowance	*6,475*
Taxable income	*53,525*
Tax	
£37,400 @ 20%	*7,480*
£16,125 @ 40%	*6,450*
Total Tax Bill	**13,930**

Example 2

The circumstances are exactly the same as above but we assume that Sandy wants to make a large pension contribution to save some tax. Let's say he has accumulated £40,000 in a savings account. He'd like to invest this money in a SIPP. Because he has earnings of £60,000 he is allowed to make a 'gross contribution' of up to £60,000 and claim full tax relief against his earnings.

Sandy's 'gross contribution' will be £50,000 (£40,000/0.80) which is less than his earnings and therefore qualifies for tax relief.

Sandy will personally invest £40,000 and the taxman will top this up with another £10,000 in basic-rate tax relief, giving him a total gross pension contribution of £50,000.

Sandy is also entitled to higher-rate relief because some of his income is taxed at 40%. To calculate his tax refund we multiply his higher rate income by 20%:

$$£16,125 \times 20\% = £3,225$$

In total Sandy has £50,000 of pension savings. He personally contributed £40,000 but got £3,225 back from the taxman so his total cost is £36,775.

Although that's a good result Sandy hasn't obtained the maximum tax relief. Maximum tax relief means getting your pension investments at a 40% discount, ie, paying just £30,000 for £50,000 of investments.

The problem is Sandy is only obtaining the maximum tax relief on a small portion of his pension contribution: the portion of his salary taxed at 40% which is £16,125. He is not receiving higher-rate tax relief on the full £50,000 contribution.

There's probably nothing Sandy can do to increase his income but he could in future spread his pension contributions across more than one tax year to ensure he receives the maximum tax relief.

Summary

The new pension contribution rules are enormously attractive to most investors and savers for the following reasons:

- You can belong to your employer's occupational pension scheme and contribute to a self-invested personal pension at the same time.

- You can contribute an amount equal to your entire annual earnings and obtain tax relief. This is fantastic for property investors who have other resources at their disposal and want to invest a large lump sum.

- It's also good news for those who earn large bonuses or other windfall payments that are usually heavily taxed.

- To enjoy the highest possible tax relief you should, however, only contribute to the extent that your earnings are taxed at 40%.

New Rules for High Earners

Income Above £100,000

Starting on 6th April 2010 you should definitely consider making pension contributions when your income rises above £100,000.

If you do, you will enjoy up to 60% tax relief!

Why? Because from 2010-11, your income tax personal allowance will be reduced by £1 for every £2 you earn above £100,000.

For example, if your income is £102,000, your income tax personal allowance will be reduced by £1,000 which means an extra £1,000 of your income will be taxed.

When your income is approximately £113,000 your personal allowance will have been completely withdrawn, increasing your tax bill by around £2,600.

However, if you contribute to a pension you will reduce your taxable income and protect your income tax personal allowance.

For example, let's say you have taxable income of £110,000 in 2010/11 and make a gross pension contribution of £100.

For starters you will receive £40 of income tax relief, as per normal. However, the pension contribution also reduces your taxable income by £100, thus preserving an extra £50 of your personal allowance and saving you an extra £20 in income tax.

In summary, your £100 pension contribution produces £60 of tax savings – a total of 60% tax relief!

Income Above £150,000

In the April 2009 Budget the Government announced a crazy clampdown on pension contributions made by high earners.

This £3 billion tax hit will affect those earning £150,000 or more but will only fully impact those earning at least £180,000.

From 6th April 2011 if you earn more than £150,000 you will have your pension tax relief gradually withdrawn. When your income is £180,000 you will only enjoy 20% tax relief.

This new attack on high earners is doubly cruel because those individuals will face a marginal tax rate of 50% from April 2010. So someone who pays tax at 50% will only save 20% by contributing to a pension.

Not much incentive, is it?

When this book was being put to bed the final rules had not been published but Revenue & Customs has published some nasty penalties to stop high earners maxing out their pension contributions before the crackdown comes into effect in 2011.

These "anti-forestalling" provisions may apply if you have earned £150,000 or more in any tax year from **2007/8** onwards.

The good news is you can still enjoy higher-rate tax relief during the current 2009/10 tax year and the 2010/11 tax year even if your income is or was £150,000 or more, *providing you continue as normal with your 'existing regular' pension contributions.*

For example, if you've been contributing £2,000 per month over the last couple of years, you can carry on doing so until April 2011 and enjoy the maximum tax relief.

By 'regular' HMRC means monthly or quarterly contributions – anything less frequent, such as lump sum annual contributions, will be caught by the anti-forestalling provisions (a serious blow to self-employed individuals and those on bonuses who make single annual pension contributions).

Having said that, those high earners who make irregular annual pension contributions will still be able to contribute between £20,000 and £30,000 per year for the next two tax years and enjoy maximum tax relief.

In summary, there is still scope for those earning £150,000 or more to enjoy higher-rate tax relief for the next couple of years – speak to your financial adviser before you act because the rules are still being drafted.

Those who have never earned more than £150,000, but expect to in future, should consider 'making hay while the sun shines' and contributing as much as possible while they can enjoy 40% tax relief.

Borrowing Limits

This was probably the most unwelcome of the A-Day changes. Pension investors can only borrow up to 50% of their net pension assets.

For example, if your gross pension contribution is £20,000 you can only borrow an extra £10,000, bringing your total property investment to £30,000.

You don't find any properties that cost £30,000 these days, which means the only way to buy whole buildings through a SIPP is by making very big cash contributions, transferring savings from other pension schemes you belong to or teaming up with other investors.

You don't need to borrow money to invest in most *property funds*, however, because the initial investment is usually modest.

Furthermore, the borrowing restriction applies to the SIPP itself but not to any investment vehicles held inside the SIPP. So pension savings can be invested in property funds that in turn borrow money to boost returns.

For example, real estate investment trusts can borrow as much money as any buy-to-let investor.

On a smaller scale, property investment firms and financial advisers have been setting up heavily geared syndicates for SIPP investors, with loan-to-value ratios of up to 75%.

Property syndicates are often structured as 'exempt property unit trusts (EPUTs). EPUTs are unregulated collective investment schemes.

They're 'exempt' because they don't have to pay any capital gains tax, provided all the investors are pension schemes. And because they're unregulated you usually have to invest via a financial adviser.

Any borrowing is undertaken by the EPUT and not at the SIPP level. The size of loan is therefore determined by what the bank and company administering the EPUT are happy with. (For more information about exempt property unit trusts go to www.consortium-im.com.)

If you can contribute £25,000 to your SIPP and invest that money in an exempt property unit trust, which in turn borrows another £75,000 to buy property, you could end up with the best of both worlds: all the pension tax reliefs plus all the benefits of a heavily geared property investment.

Please note that there aren't many heavily geared syndicates available to property investors at present. Most SIPP providers and companies structuring property investments for pension investors remain quite tight lipped about exactly how much money can be borrowed, possibly for fear of a clamp down by the Government. However, it's an area worth watching closely for future developments.

It's also essential to make sure you deal only with a reputable SIPP provider to ensure that the investment complies fully with the pension regulations.

Lifetime Allowance

The lifetime allowance is the maximum amount of money you are allowed to accumulate inside pension funds. Exceed the lifetime cap and you get fined – the Government hates it when wealthy people save tax!

The cap for people retiring in the 2009/2010 tax year is £1.75 million. This will rise to £1.8 million in 2010/2011. No further increase is currently anticipated until at least 2016.

If your pension pot exceeds this lifetime limit, either through hard saving or successful investment decisions, there is a 25% tax charge on the surplus assets. You will also be allowed to take these extra funds as a cash lump sum. Doing so, however, will result in a 55% tax charge.

Retirement Age

A new minimum retirement age will be introduced from April 2010. From that date 55 will be the minimum age at which you can start taking benefits from a pension.

This rule will apply to both occupational and personal pension schemes such as SIPPs.

When you hit the minimum retirement age you are able to start receiving a pension without having to retire from your job. This could enable you to withdraw from work gradually and combine work and retirement.

Tax-free Lump Sums

Since 2006, members of *any* pension fund (both occupational pension funds and SIPPs) have been able to take 25% of their pension savings as a tax-free cash lump sum when they hit the minimum retirement age.

It's important to stress that you cannot directly access the remaining 75% of your money. This will eventually have to be used to generate some type of regular pension (see below).

More Choice & Flexibility When You Retire

One of the major drawbacks of the old pension rules was the lack of flexibility when you started withdrawing benefits. When you reached the age of 75 you had to buy an annuity with most of your pension savings.

Since A-Day there is a bit more flexibility. You are no longer forced to buy a traditional annuity when you hit 75. Instead you can pay yourself a new type of retirement income called Alternatively Secured Pension (ASP).

No matter what method you use, it's important to remember that money withdrawn from your pension is fully taxed. Furthermore, you have to pay tax on withdrawals of both income and capital. This makes pension income the most heavily taxed type of income.

On the plus side, however, you can take 25% of your savings as a tax-free lump sum and many retirees only pay tax at the basic rate (20%), so the pension 'sting in the tail' isn't always as sharp as it looks.

Income Before Age 75

Between the ages of 55 and 75 you will be able to leave your pension savings fully invested and keep making contributions. However, if you want to start withdrawing money you do this in one of two ways:

- **Buy an Annuity.** Annuities were discussed in detail in Chapter 13. Although annuities lack flexibility, the income from them is often far higher than from alternative investments. Furthermore, annuities remain the only way to guarantee your income for life. They will therefore continue to be the only practical option for retirees who need a high and secure income.

- **Unsecured Income** (also known as income drawdown). If you want to get your hands on your tax-free lump sum but don't want any other income at this stage, or if you want to be able to vary your income to suit your needs you can opt for unsecured income.

  You don't have to withdraw any income but if you do, the maximum you can extract from your pension pot is broadly equal to 120% of the annuity your fund could buy. You can opt for a traditional annuity at any time. Furthermore, provided you don't put all your savings into unsecured income you can continue making contributions and claiming tax relief.

This flexibility gives you a lot of scope to do constructive tax planning. For example, if you're still working and paying tax at 40%, you may prefer to keep the majority of your pension money invested in a completely tax-free environment.

Income After Age 75

Before April 2006 you had to buy an annuity when you reached 75. Nowadays you can either buy an annuity or take alternatively secured pension (ASP).

The Government has clamped down on some of the ASP rules. These new rules were designed to prevent wealthier retirees passing their pension savings to their heirs. It's important to point out, however, that ASP has not been scrapped and you still don't have to buy an annuity when you are 75.

The maximum income you can take is lower than for unsecured income and there is a minimum income you are required to draw. You will have to pay yourself a distribution which is broadly no less that 55% but no more than 90% of a comparable annuity for a 75-year-old.

This calculation is reviewed annually but the amount of income is likely to always be lower than for a conventional annuity and the gap will increase as you get older. So ASP will not be a good choice for people who need to maximize their retirement income. It does, however, offer greater flexibility than an annuity because you can:

- Vary your level of income.

- Defer buying an annuity if you think rates will improve.

- Buy an annuity with some or all of your pension savings at any time.

- Keep your money invested in growth assets and draw an income at the same time.

Although you can vary your income under ASP there's not much incentive to keep your savings invested for too long. If you die with surplus pension savings, up to 82% of this money will ultimately go to the Government, not your children.

Scheme Pensions

A new option offered by a small number of providers is a Scheme Pension. This allows you to withdraw a higher income than would be available under ASP. Furthermore the income can be guaranteed for up to 10 years. So if the pension scheme member dies the income will continue to be paid to beneficiaries.

Any remaining funds can be transferred to other members of the scheme who can access them without paying excessive tax penalties when they themselves reach pensionable age.

Theses schemes are generally designed mainly for wealthier individuals (those with at least £200,000 of pension assets) because the initial set up costs are at least £1,000 and annual charges run to hundreds of pounds.

There are concerns that HM Revenue & Customs will clamp down on these arrangements if they are seen as inheritance tax avoidance tools.

For more information:

- Axa Winterthur Family Suntrust – axawinterthur.co.uk
- Rowanmoor Family Pension Trust – rowanmoor.co.uk
- Hornbuckle Mitchell – www.hornbucklemitchell.co.uk

Selling Existing Property to Your Pension Fund

Before A-Day you could not sell property you already owned to your pension plan. You can now.

This change is welcomed mostly by business owners who want to transfer their company premises to their SIPPs.

Of course, the crucial question is whether the costs of doing this outweigh the benefits. Selling property to a SIPP will generate a capital gains tax bill so you will have to weigh up your expected gains (pension tax reliefs) against all the costs (a capital gains tax bill, selling fees, stamp duty etc).

Summary

Apart from offering tremendous tax benefits such as tax relief on contributions and tax-free investment returns, pension plans have become much more flexible since April 2006:

- You can now belong to both your employer's pension fund and a personal pension plan.

- You can make large tax-favoured pension contributions that vary considerably from year to year. This makes it easy for you to get bonuses, inheritances and other windfalls into a tax-sheltered investment plan.

- You will be able to carry on working and draw benefits from your company's pension scheme.

- Before you reach the age of 75 you can draw a high income from your pension pot and keep control over your wealth.

- After you reach the age of 75 you can still defer buying an annuity and take a more flexible alternatively secured pension instead.

Chapter 15

What Kind of Property Can You Put in a SIPP?

Prologue
Sunday, December 4th 2005, Downing St

Gordon: Tony, I've decided to ban residential property from SIPPs in tomorrow's speech.

Tony: Thanks for the warning but blimey that's short notice. Cherie and I were just about to put deposits down on two new flats in Birmingham.

Gordon: Haven't you heard? New flats are dropping like ninepins these days. So maybe I've done you a favour... perhaps you'll do one for me in the near future.

Tony: Why the change of heart? I thought this was our idea.

Gordon: Aye, it was but I just couldn't stomach the thought of all those City Fat Cats buying holiday homes on the Costas and what have you. Making money's one thing but enjoying yourself at the same time is intolerable.

Tony: But most people probably just wanted to buy investment properties, like Cherie and I. Couldn't you have done something a bit less radical – I don't know, ban overseas property instead? After all nobody wants to buy a holiday home in Boring Britain.

Gordon: Personally, I always enjoy my Scottish winter breaks. I've never seen the attraction of lording it up in an Italian villa.

Tony: Yes all right, Gordon. So where does all this leave me and Cherie? In the near future we're going to be raking in money from public speaking engagements. It would be quite handy if we could save some tax. How do we invest our pension savings now?

Gordon: Have you thought about Government bonds? After all, we could use all the money we can get.

Tony: Personally, I wouldn't touch bonds with a barge pole – Cherie and I like our investments a bit more racy.

Gordon: Shares then.

Tony: Crikey, I said racy. I didn't say I wanted to play the lottery. Have you forgotten how much we lost investing in Dot Bomb shares?

Gordon: Yes, I remember being very upset for you. Well, then you'll be pleased to know I haven't banned all property. It's OK to invest in property you cannot enjoy personally.

Tony: Oh well, that's fine then. There's no way we'd enjoy using a flat in Birmingham.

Gordon: No, Tony, that's not what I meant. From now on you can only invest in indirect property.

Tony: What do you mean by 'indirect'? Sounds a bit like your answers to tricky Budget questions.

Gordon: Ha ha, very funny, Tony. What I mean is you and Cherie can put your SIPP money in property funds like REITs. This will let you invest in a big spread of professionally managed properties.

Tony: Now you're talking my sort of language. How do I get my hands on these 'reets'.

Gordon: There aren't any.

Tony: Oh.

Gordon: Don't worry. We'll be introducing legislation in 2006 that will get the ball rolling.

Tony: Is there any other way I can invest in 'indirect property'?

Gordon: Other property funds will be fine too. I'm just trying to slap together a few rules this afternoon.

Tony: Plus ça change, plus la même chose.

Gordon: Oh shut up, Tony.

The Present Day

In December 2005 the Government announced that pension savers would be barred from putting their money in residential property. In his pre-Budget speech Gordon Brown said that "anti-avoidance and fraud measures published today will address the misuse of SIPPS schemes to purchase second homes."

Before Mr Brown made his announcement it would have been possible to buy your holiday villa in Tuscany at a 40% discount paid for by the taxman. Companies promoting overseas property made a big play of this opportunity and aggressively promoted using SIPPs to buy second homes after A-Day.

This is precisely what the Government didn't like and why the loophole was closed. They want your money to be invested only in assets you cannot use personally. So out go antiques, art and classic cars too.

But the property ban went much further than 'second homes'. With the stroke of a pen our political masters also banned all traditional buy-to-let property investments as well.

The penalties are ferocious. If a SIPP owns taxable property the member has to pay an initial fine of 40% to 55% of the amount invested and the scheme administrator faces an additional 15% fine.

So what kind of property CAN you put in your pension? As it turns out the new rules are not as bad as many feared.

You can still put many different types of property in a SIPP – including certain types of residential property – and enjoy all the pension tax reliefs.

In this chapter were going to take a closer look at what the new rules allow – exactly what types of property you can and cannot stick in your pension fund.

Then we're going to take a look at what is happening out there in the real world – what sort of property investments are being offered by pension providers and property fund managers.

What is Taxable Property?

SIPPs are only subject to penalties if they invest in 'taxable property'. Taxable property includes:

- Residential property, and
- 'Tangible moveable property'

Tangible moveable property includes virtually anything that you can touch and move: works of art, fine wines, rare stamps, yachts and other goodies investors had originally hoped to buy using the taxman's money. (Gold bugs will be relieved to hear, however, that the ban does not include investment-grade bullion.)

Residential property is defined as "a building that is used or suitable for use as a dwelling". Apart from the obvious candidates – flats and houses – residential property includes:

- The gardens and grounds of a residential property (and any other buildings on the land)

- Hotels that provide accommodation rights

- Timeshares

- Beach huts

Some types of property have slipped through the net and are specifically excluded from the definition of residential property (ie you can put them in your SIPP):

- Children's homes

- Student halls of residence

- Nursing homes

- Personal care homes for those suffering from a disability, drink or drugs problem or a mental illness.

- Hospitals and hospices

- Prisons

Parts of Buildings

Where it becomes confusing is where a building has both a residential and commercial element. For example, the taxman has indicated that where a building includes a shop with a separate flat above (ie a flat with a separate entrance) the property will be treated as two separate buildings.

The flat will be treated as residential property and the shop as commercial property.

When it is necessary to determine whether part or all of a building is a dwelling (ie not allowed inside a SIPP), Revenue & Customs has stated that it will look at the facts of each case and take a "pragmatic and commonsense approach".

If there is mixed use then what matters most is the primary use of the property. For example, if a dentist uses two rooms in a house as a dental surgery the property will be residential property as it is suitable for use as a dwelling.

Student Halls

Allowing student halls into SIPPs has caused quite a stir. Student flats are often extremely lucrative investments offering above-average rental yields and a stable and reliable income.

It's important to point out, however, that you cannot simply buy a flat, rent it out to students and claim all the pension tax breaks. You also cannot buy a share in a big block of flats that is rented out to students.

In August 2006, Revenue & Customs issued a newsletter explaining what it means by the term 'student halls'.

The property needs to be *connected* to an educational establishment and provide accommodation only for students of that establishment.

The taxman lists the following features that indicate whether a property is a proper hall of residence:

- The university identifies the property as one of its halls of residence.

- The university helps place students in the building.

- The students come from the same university.

- The building is not broken up into self-contained apartments.

- There are common living areas or cooking facilities.

The first two requirements represent the biggest hurdle for pension investors wanting to set up their own student halls – you cannot set up a student hall without co-operation from the university in question.

Clearly a block of flats that is merely rented out to students will not necessarily be a 'hall of residence'.

Hotels

If a pension scheme owns a whole hotel or is a joint owner of a whole hotel then this is not regarded as residential property.

In this circumstance the hotel is treated as commercial property. In other words, you can stick it in your SIPP and claim all the tax breaks.

Hotel investments are only treated as taxable residential property in cases of part ownership (for example where you own a single room) and you have a right to stay in that room or another room for free or at a reduced rate or if you have timeshare rights (for example, the right to stay in the room for two weeks in July).

Job-Related Property

Also exempt from the taxable property rules are certain types of 'job-related' property. For example, if the property is occupied by an employee who is required, as a condition of his employment contract, to live in the property. A good example would be a caretaker's flat.

The employee must not be a member of the pension scheme or connected to another member or the employer.

Residential property is also exempt if it is used in connection with business premises.

A good example would be a shop with a flat above that is leased to the person trading out of the shop. The tenant must not be a member of the pension scheme or connected to the member. The property immediately becomes taxable if these conditions cease to apply.

Property Funds & Syndicates

The Government doesn't have a problem with residential property per se. What it was dreading after A-Day were headlines like:

Taxpayer Foots Bill for Luxury Holiday Villas

Hence the clamp-down on any type of residential property that you can enjoy personally.

However, the 2006 Finance Act does allow you to invest your pension savings in residential property if you do so through a "genuinely diverse commercial vehicle".

This opens the door for investment in certain types of residential property funds and property syndicates.

So what exactly is a "genuinely diverse commercial vehicle"?

The new rules contain a number of tests that have to be passed to qualify for the pension tax breaks, including:

- Each investor must own 10% or less – ie there must be 10 or more investors in the fund or syndicate.

- No personal use of property is allowed by the investor or connected persons (spouses and other close relatives).

- The total value of the properties must be at least £1 million or there must be at least three properties.

- No single residential property must represent more than 40% of the total assets.

- If the vehicle is a company it must not be a close company (generally five or fewer shareholders).

Summary

So what do these new rules mean in practice to the average SIPP investor?

- For starters, we know that only *residential* property is banned. A residential property is one that is used as a dwelling (home) or is *suitable* for use as a dwelling. Non-residential property – in other words commercial property – still qualifies for SIPP investment.

- The commercial property funds discussed in Part 2 (REITs, property unit trusts and investment companies) can all be put in your SIPP.

- Most bricks and mortar commercial property investments are easily identified as such. They include high street shops, offices in established office buildings, warehouses and industrial units. These all qualify for pension tax breaks.

- However, there are instances where a building may have a residential *and* commercial component or where a residential property that is suitable as a dwelling is used as an office without many modifications being made. In these circumstances you are at the taxman's mercy and all or part of the property may be classified as taxable residential property.

- The legislation specifically mentions certain types of 'quasi-residential property'. Allowed are university-recognised student halls, nursing and care homes, hospitals and prisons. Certain hotel investments are also allowed provided the investment does not come with accommodation rights. Banned from your SIPP are timeshares and my personal favourite, beach huts.

- Residential property (flats and houses) is still allowed provided the investment takes place through a "genuinely diverse commercial vehicle". This includes residential REITs (although there aren't any at the time of writing) and other vehicles such as property funds and syndicates that have 10 or more members, at least £1 million of assets or three properties and prohibit private use by investors.

SIPP Property Investments in Practice

Although we know what types of property the taxman lets you put in your SIPP, the critical question is, what type of property can you include *in practice*?

Prisons may be allowed but how does the average investor go about investing in one? The same goes for hotels, student halls, and nursing homes.

And what about these "genuinely diverse commercial vehicles"? How exactly do you go about finding one?

Let's start with the two simplest property investments you can put in your SIPP: bricks-and-mortar commercial property, REITs and property unit trusts.

SIPP investors have been buying traditional bricks-and-mortar commercial properties for years so this is a well-established route.

To invest directly in commercial property all you have to do is pick a property you like, go along to one of the established SIPP providers and, if the property is suitable, they will set the ball in motion. (See Chapter 16 for more info on choosing a SIPP provider.)

The biggest obstacle to overcome is probably funding. With only very restricted borrowings allowed (50% of your net pension assets), most SIPP investors who buy whole commercial properties will have to either make large cash contributions, transfer money from other pension schemes or team up with other investors.

It's even easier to invest in real estate investment trusts and property unit trusts through your SIPP. This can usually be done online at the click of a mouse.

AIM Companies

There are numerous property companies quoted on the Alternative Investment Market (AIM).

You are not allowed to shelter these investments inside an ISA but you can invest in them through a SIPP.

They are not true tax shelters because the companies themselves are liable to pay corporation tax on their rental income and capital gains.

However, any income and capital gains you personally enjoy as a shareholder can be sheltered from the taxman.

Two of the most respected AIM property companies, set up to profit from weakness in the property market are:

- Max Property – maxpropertygroup.com
- London & Stamford – londonandstamford.com

Max Property was set up in mid-2009 and is the brainchild of Nick Leslau who, according to the *Sunday Times* Rich List, has built a £200 million fortune through shrewd investments in property.

Leslau managed to poach Helical Bar's Mike Brown as chief executive and says deals must show an initial return of 25-30 per cent to even be considered.

The company's strategy is to *"exploit the current cyclical weakness in the real estate market, in particular through opportunistic acquisitions, active asset management and judicious use of non-recourse finance to enhance shareholder returns."*

In July 2009 the company was reported to be in talks to buy a portfolio of distressed industrial properties from the receivers of collapsed industrial firm Industrious.

London & Stamford has been around a bit longer and is headed by veteran property investors Raymond Mould and Patrick Vaughan.

In July 2009 it announced that it had raised over £200 million to exploit big discounts in the commercial property market. The company is also considering moving to the main London Stock Exchange and converting to a REIT.

The company kept its powder dry when property prices were collapsing in 2007 and 2008. It raised £248 million in November 2007 but delayed making any acquisitions until 2009, having considered 200 potential purchases along the way.

SIPP Funds & Syndicates

Apart from property unit trusts and stock exchange quoted property companies (REITs, property investment companies and AIM companies), there are several smaller property funds and property syndicates available to private investors. Typically these are not regulated by the Financial Services Authority.

They take various legal forms, such as "exempt property unit trusts", "limited liability partnerships" and "open-ended investment companies".

SIPPs are allowed to invest in them but they're mostly banned from ISAs. To avoid confusing these funds with the big property funds discussed in earlier chapters, I'll refer to these investments as "SIPP funds" in the pages that follow.

SIPP funds come in all shapes and sizes: most invest in commercial property but some invest in residential. Some invest in UK property, others invest overseas. Some are offered by well-known firms with established track records, others are offered by relative newcomers.

SIPP funds offer many of the benefits of REITs and authorised property trusts outlined in Chapter 4. For example, the minimum investment, though higher, is usually far less than you would pay to buy a property outright. For example the minimum investment will typically range from £5,000 to £50,000.

SIPP funds are also completely passive investments, requiring no time or effort from the investor and some reduce risk by holding a spread of properties in their portfolios (although many will own a single property only).

On the downside, most SIPP funds and syndicates are far less liquid than REITs and authorised property unit trusts. In other words, you will often find it difficult to sell your investment quickly.

Many SIPP funds also have significant borrowings which is either an advantage or a disadvantage, depending on your point of view.

For example, in July 2009 *Property Week* magazine announced that Pinder Fry & Benjamin's regional offices fund was to be placed into liquidation after breaching its loan covenants. The fund was launched in 2007 to buy unlet office buildings and raised money from SIPP investors.

Most SIPP funds are not directly available to private investors. The companies that set them up will usually only deal with financial advisers. This can make it quite difficult to do any initial research because many of the websites contain only limited information.

In fact, a bit like CS Lewis's *The Lion, The Witch and The Wardrobe*, there seems to be a whole hidden world of investment opportunities that only a select few know about.

However, an excellent way to find out about new launches and offerings is to subscribe to a good property investment magazine like *Property Week* (www.propertyweek.com).

Note that even if an investment qualifies for SIPP inclusion, that doesn't necessarily mean your SIPP provider will let you invest. For example, some will only accept investment in property syndicates if all the investors are under the same SIPP provider's roof.

In the next section I'm going to take a brief look at some of the residential and commercial SIPP funds available to private investors.

Please note that these are definitely NOT investment recommendations. I'm only writing about these specific offerings to give you some idea of what's on offer in the real world.

Most of the funds that were around before the collapse of the property market have not fared well. Some have been liquidated, some have been forced to sell properties at knockdown prices to reduce their debts and some have stopped investors from selling their holdings so as to preserve cash.

So it really is a case of Buyer Beware.

SIPP Funds

Here are some examples of SIPP funds aimed at private investors:

- Eaton Investment Management (eatoninvest.com) has launched a special opportunities fund targeting returns of 20% per year. The fund will invest in *"low density, income-producing properties that can benefit from planning gains and the application of active asset management techniques"*. The fund is looking to raise £8 million equity to which it will add £12 million of debt. The minimum investment is £50,000 and is targeted at SIPP investors.

- Cavendish & Gloucester has launched a land fund so private investors can buy land that has planning permission at deep discounts from cash starved builders.

- Braemar Group (braemar-group.co.uk) has launched several funds for SIPP investors including a ground rents fund and a student accommodation fund, both listed on the

Channel Islands Stock Exchange. Both funds have a minimum investment of £10,000 and, according to the company, qualify for inclusion in SIPPs and ISAs.

- Coral Portfolio (coralportfolio.com) has set up an ungeared fund of funds for private investors who want to invest in existing student accommodation funds.

- Cordea Savills (cordeasavills.com) manages a selection of private investor funds including a Student Hall Fund and a Diversified Residential Opportunities Fund.

- London Central Portfolio (londoncentralportfolio.com) has launched a vulture fund called The Recovery Fund to invest exclusively in prime residential areas like Knightsbridge and Mayfair. It will renovate the properties and let them out. The fund is targeting returns of 15% per year. The minimum investment is £50,000.

- EPH Partners has launched a fund to invest in pre-let residential property in Sweden (ephpartners.com/sverige). The minimum investment is £10,000 and the fund is targeting returns of 12% per year.

- Property First Asset Management (propertyfirstassets.com) has launched a vulture fund to buy repossessed property.

- Residential Property Asset Management (rpamfunds.co.uk) has launched the Residential Property Recovery Fund, focusing on property outside London: *"RPR offers the opportunity to acquire residential property whilst sentiment is weak; with prices at near 50% discounts to 2007 prices, at close to build cost, at discounts to RICS valuations of circa 20%, and with gross yields of 8% plus."* The minimum investment is £25,000.

- Assetz (assetz.co.uk) has launched a fund investing in UK, US and Spanish distressed residential property and is aiming to buy assets at a 30-70% discount.

- Property Bourse (www.propertybourse.com) allows you to buy and sell holdings in property syndicates.

Chapter 16

How to Set Up and Run Your Own Property SIPP

Introduction

The advantage of SIPPs over other personal pensions is simply greater *investment flexibility*. SIPP investors get to manage their investments themselves and can create a portfolio consisting of:

- Cash and government and corporate bonds
- Shares
- Unit trusts and investment trusts
- Commercial property
- Property funds and syndicates, including residential funds

Who Offers Property SIPPs?

The number of SIPP providers has exploded in recent years. If you want to invest in real estate investment trusts or property unit trusts you don't have to go to a specialist provider. You can use one of the low-cost online providers such as the Hargreaves Lansdown Vantage SIPP (www.h-l.co.uk). This has no set-up fee and very low ongoing fees. Other alternatives include Fidelity Funds Network (fundsnetwork.co.uk) or Killik (www.killik.com).

Not all SIPP providers allow you to invest in direct property and unregulated funds and syndicates, however. Those that specialize in property SIPPs include:

- Suffolk Life - www.suffolklife.co.uk
- James Hay - www.jameshay.co.uk
- AJ Bell - www.ajbell.co.uk
- Pointon York - www.sippsolutions.com
- Hornbuckle Mitchell – www.hornbuckle.co.uk
- Talbot and Muir - www.talbotmuir.co.uk

You'll find lots of info about property SIPPs on these websites.

Table 7
James Hay – SIPP Fees

Set-up Fees:
* Property transaction fee: £550 +0.1% over £400,000

Ongoing Fees:
* Annual Property Administration Charge: £500 for each letting
* Annual Mortgage Administration Charge: £100

How Much Do SIPPs Cost?

The main drawback of bricks and mortar property SIPPs is the fees. The costs are higher because they are 'bespoke' investments, rather than off-the-shelf investment products.

You will have to pay both set-up fees and ongoing fees. Set-up fees include the SIPP administrator's fee and the same costs you incur when buying any property: legal fees, surveyor's fees, lender's fees etc.

Ongoing fees include the SIPP administrator's charges, surveyor's fees, property management company fees and legal fees. All these fees will normally be paid out of your SIPP bank account and not from your own pocket. You may also end up paying fees to your IFA.

To give you some idea of the actual costs, above in Table 7 are the fees of a well-known SIPP administrator. They're by no means meant to be representative but do serve as a good starting point.

Transferring Savings from Existing Pensions

Apart from pension contributions another way of getting money into a property SIPP is to make transfers from your *existing* pension savings. If you've worked for more than one employer over the years there's a good chance you'll have accumulated pension rights in one or more occupational schemes. Most SIPP providers will let you transfer these rights, plus any savings you've accumulated in personal pension plans.

This is one of the easiest ways of getting a large lump sum into your SIPP. Pension transfers have become extremely popular in recent years as more and more investors seek to give their pension savings a new lease of life.

There are several reasons you may wish to transfer from an old pension scheme to a new SIPP:

- To consolidate all your pension savings under one roof.

- To benefit from wider investment choice.

- Because you don't trust your old occupational pension schemes to meet their promises, for example if the company goes bust and there is a pension deficit.

- Because you feel you can personally grow your pension savings better and achieve a higher pension than you would be entitled to from your existing pension arrangements.

- To escape high charges from existing pension schemes.

The key is to ensure that the benefits you hope to enjoy are greater than the benefits you might lose from your old pension arrangements. You also have to take account of any exit penalties and professional adviser fees or commissions for handling the transfer to your new pension.

It's important to stress that you *must* take professional advice and not rush into making a transfer. You're probably better off with an adviser who charges a fee rather than one who charges a commission. If the advice is on a commission basis the adviser will only receive payment if a transfer actually takes place. This may sway the advice in favour of making such a transfer.

When calculating the amount allowed to be transferred, the pension scheme trustees will decide if they should take account of discretionary benefits such as pension increases – in most cases they don't. The cash value usually doesn't provide for lump sum death benefits, widows' pensions or dependants' pensions. So if you transfer you could lose these valuable discretionary benefits.

A 'critical yield' is calculated that shows how fast your new SIPP will have to grow, eg 7% per year, to match the benefits of your old pension. Here are some further transfer dos and don'ts:

- Don't transfer from your *current* employer's occupational pension into which both you and your employer contribute. Many companies contribute over 15% to final salary schemes and on average 6.5% to defined contribution schemes. By transferring you would lose this 'free money'.

- Don't transfer from public-sector pension schemes. These are the blue chips of pension schemes, offering full inflation protection and other benefits.

- Check out the death benefits of your former pension scheme, which may not be matched by a personal pension scheme without having to buy a life insurance policy.

- Don't bother transferring if you have just a small amount of money in your former pension. It's arguably only worth transferring if you have more than £10,000 invested.

- It may be reckless and expensive to transfer if you are less than 10 years away from retirement.

- If you transfer from a final salary scheme to a SIPP you give up the promise of a fixed level of pension income and are now dependent on how well you can grow your money. You will also have to pay the costs of running the plan.

In summary, you may have a lot to gain by transferring savings from old pension plans to a SIPP, especially if you are many years away from retirement and believe you can grow your investments faster than most pension fund managers. Pension transfers are one of the easiest ways of getting money into a SIPP.

However, you also potentially have a lot to lose if your existing pension funds offer a variety of benefits that will be taken away and if the transfer charges are high.

SIPP Property Purchases in Practice

To give you some idea how bricks and mortar property SIPPs are set up and run, and some of the rules and regulations, I've compiled the following beginners' guide. Most of the information comes from the existing providers websites.

Bullet points and diagrams are used to make the information easy to read and digest:

- The first thing you have to do is set up your SIPP account with your chosen provider – this usually requires evidence of your earnings and completion of an application form.

- Next you submit details of the property in which you're interested by filling out a property questionnaire. The SIPP provider will have to decide if the property complies with Revenue & Customs and other requirements.

- A surveyor's report is arranged to determine the suitability of the property. These fees are paid out of your SIPP account.

- Often, but not always, the SIPP provider's own solicitors will be used to carry out the purchase of the property.

- All legal fees, stamp duty and other set-up costs will also be paid out of your SIPP account. Each SIPP has its very own bank account so you can keep track of where the money's going. This makes them very transparent investment products.

How a Typical Property SIPP Works

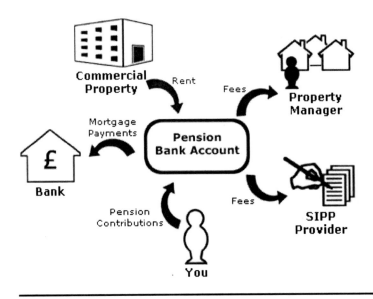

- You have to ensure that there is enough money to buy the property and cover all costs before the purchase goes ahead. Payment can come from new pension contributions, transfers from your existing pension funds and bank borrowings.

- You will have to arrange the borrowings yourself but the loan will be in the name of the pension trustees who will have to be satisfied that there is sufficient income to meet the loan repayments and other costs.

- The lender must be a proper commercial lender (in other words, not a member of your family or a friend).

- The loan will typically be on an interest and capital repayment basis.

- The lender has to accept that the SIPP administrator's liability for the loan is limited to just the sale value of the property. The loan will also not be acceptable if it requires a guarantee from you, the SIPP holder.

- The pension trustees, typically an offshoot of the SIPP administrator, will be the legal owners of the property and the landlord, not you.

- A formal lease must be entered into at the time of completion unless there is already one in place.

- The lease must be for a minimum period, for example five years. It may have to be for a longer term if there is borrowing – the lender may require the lease to be as long as the mortgage period.

- The SIPP provider is usually responsible for managing the property and usually appoints a professional property management company to do this.

- To cover this, an annual property administration fee is paid out of your SIPP bank account.

- The SIPP administrator is usually responsible for making sure the building is properly insured because it is the legal owner.

- If your company occupies the property, the letting must be on commercial terms – you cannot overpay to get extra money into your SIPP or underpay to make life easy for your business.

- Development of a property can be undertaken from within a SIPP.

- Most SIPP providers allow a single property purchase by multiple SIPP members – a form of property syndicate. This can save on costs because there will be only one set of property purchase costs.

- Typically a central bank account is set up to receive the rents and pay the mortgage and surplus funds are then distributed to each SIPP member.

- The partnership agreement should cover what happens on death, retirement and when new partners join.

A Typical SIPP Property Purchase

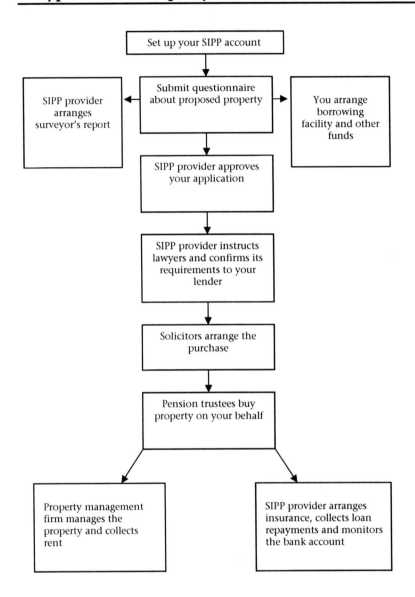

Part 4

Bricks & Mortar
vs
Property Pensions
vs
ISAs

Chapter 17

ISAs vs Bricks and Mortar: Detailed Example

Introduction

As we've seen, there are many differences between putting your money in a property fund ISA and investing directly in property.

Some of the benefits of direct property will appeal to certain types of investors, while some of the benefits of indirect property ISAs will appeal to others.

For example, owning part of a large portfolio of properties will appeal to some investors; others would prefer to scout for property themselves in the hope of picking up a genuine bargain.

Some investors will like not having to be a landlord with all the responsibility this entails; others like the idea of investing in 'proper' bricks and mortar rather than property fund units or shares.

There's no right or wrong way to invest in property – only what's right for you.

And it's not an all-or-nothing decision – you can invest in both property funds and direct property!

In my opinion, the two most important differences between property ISAs and direct property investments are the following:

- Property ISA returns are completely tax free.
- You can personally borrow to invest in direct property.

ISAs, therefore, have one major advantage and one major disadvantage: all returns are tax free but you cannot boost your returns using gearing. For many investors not being able to gear up the investment would be seen as a serious drawback.

The traditional 'buy-to-let' model is based on the principle that by borrowing lots of money you get to enjoy the capital appreciation on a much bigger chunk of real estate than you could otherwise afford.

The great thing is that even if property prices are rising very slowly you can still make good money out of traditional buy to let – what I call turning 5% per year into 15% per year.

There are risks involved, the most important one being that property prices might fall.

In these circumstances you will suffer from 'reverse gearing' and a relatively modest drop in property prices could wipe out most if not all of your equity.

The second major danger is that the property will lie empty and there will be no rental income to cover your mortgage and other expenses.

Investing in a property ISA is arguably less risky because no personal borrowings are involved.

However, there are certain unique risks attached to this type of investment.

In particular, if you invest in stock exchange quoted property funds like REITs, the share price could fall sharply if there is a sudden loss of confidence in the property sector. Financial assets tend to be more volatile than real assets.

So which investment is likely to deliver superior returns? If everything goes according to plan does heavy gearing generate more wealth for the investor? Or do the tax savings and income payouts enjoyed by property ISA investors produce greater returns?

The only way to answer this question is to follow two investors over a period of time, one investing in a property ISA, the other investing in traditional buy-to-let.

I think the results of this case study make fascinating reading.

Case Study – Carl & Isabel

Carl and Isabel each have £21,000 to invest. Carl decides to put his money in a tax-free property ISA. Isabel decides to use her money as a deposit for a £70,000 share in a commercial property and borrows the remaining £49,000. The example is based on the following assumptions:

- Although the maximum ISA investment is £7,200 for the current tax year we can assume that Carl has already accumulated some ISA savings.

- Carl earns a combined return (income and capital growth) of 10% per year. This return is completely tax free inside an ISA. All income distributions are reinvested.

- Isabel enjoys capital gains of 5% per year. All of her rental income goes towards paying interest charges and other landlord expenses.

Let's assume Carl and Isabel hold on to their investment for 10 years and then sell up and use their savings to generate income. Their investments are summarised in Table 8.

Table 8
Property ISA vs Direct Property

End of Year	Direct Property	Property ISA
1	73,500	23,100
2	77,175	25,410
3	81,034	27,951
4	85,085	30,746
5	89,340	33,821
6	93,807	37,203
7	98,497	40,923
8	103,422	45,015
9	108,593	49,517
10	114,023	54,469

All of Isabel's rental income is eaten up by interest charges and other property letting expenses. However, she enjoys capital growth on a much larger chunk of property than Carl, the ISA investor.

After just one year her property investment has risen by 5% and is worth £73,500. Her investment grows nice and steadily in this fashion until after 10 years it is worth £114,023.

And what about Carl the ISA investor? At the beginning of the period he has just £21,000 to invest. However, his rental income does not get eaten up in loan repayments and other expenses. After one year he has enjoyed a 10% combined return equal to £2,100.

Isabel is doing much better at this stage – her capital gain in year one is £3,500 versus Carl's total return of £2,100. But Carl's investment is permanently sheltered from tax.

Furthermore, Carl's higher combined returns eventually start to catch up with Isabel – this is the power of compound interest at work: he is reinvesting his rents and this money is generating further rental income and capital growth.

After 10 years Carl's property ISA is worth £54,469. It's clear that he has made up a fair bit of ground on Isabel. Ten years ago his property investment was one-third the size of hers; now it is almost half as big.

Time to Sell Up

Carl and Isabel now decide to sell their property investments and put the proceeds into alternative high-income assets. When Carl sells his property ISA there will be no capital gains tax so he will be left with the full £54,469.

What about Isabel? She has invested outside an ISA so when she sells up her profits will be subject to capital gains tax.

Some of her profits will be tax free thanks to her annual CGT exemption. The rest will be taxed at 18%.

The CGT bill is calculated as follows:

	£
Proceeds	*114,023*
Less: Original cost	*70,000*
Gain	**44,023**
Less: CGT exemption*	*12,000*
Taxable gain	*32,023*
Tax @ 18%	**5,764**

* Estimated

So from her £114,023 property sale we have to deduct £5,764 tax and, don't forget, £49,000 in borrowings to leave her with £59,259.

In summary, Carl the ISA investor ends up with £54,469 and Isabel the direct investor ends up with £59,259. So Isabel has managed to accumulate more wealth than Carl... but not a huge amount more.

However, that's not the end of the story. What we must not lose sight of is the fact that:

- Isabel may have more money but she had to borrow money (take more risks) to get to where she is. Furthermore,

- Carl has less money but his savings are still inside an ISA and enjoying complete protection from the taxman.

Let's say Carl and Isabel put their money into income-focused investments and earn 5% per year. Because she is a higher-rate taxpayer Isabel will end up with:

£59,259 x 5% - 40% income tax = £1,778

Carl, on the other hand, will not pay any income tax so his income will be:

£54,469 x 5% = £2,723

Carl the property ISA investor ends up with 53% more money than Isabel the heavily geared property investor.

I find this result fascinating. Although borrowing money to invest in property is risky you would expect to earn superior returns if everything goes to plan.

In this case the ISA's tax benefits have ruled the day and turned a less risky investment into one that is more profitable as well.

This example shows that:

Having *less* money inside an ISA is often much better than having *more* money outside an ISA.

Like all examples a number of assumptions were made in obtaining the above result. None of these assumptions is all that unrealistic in my opinion but changing them will change the outcome. For example:

- **Rental profits.** I assumed that Isabel, the direct property investor, makes no rental profits over the whole 10-year period. You could argue that over time rents will rise but borrowing costs will probably remain static so a rental profit will emerge at some stage.

  Comment: This is true but most investment properties make a loss in the early years, something we did not inflict on Isabel in this example. Furthermore, managing a property portfolio is a time-consuming business, even if you use a letting agent. Time is money and so we could treat any rental profit as remuneration for Isabel's time.

- **Capital gains tax.** Isabel won't have to pay any capital gains tax if she simply holds on to the property and uses it to generate rental income.

  Comment: True but she'll still have to find a lump sum from somewhere to pay back her interest-only mortgage. Furthermore, no investment should be held indefinitely, including property. Investors should have the flexibility to sell and reinvest in more lucrative opportunities from time to time. As it happens, even without any CGT her income will still be just £1,951 and much less than Carl's.

- **Property price rises**. I assumed that property prices appreciate by just 5% per year. If they rise by more this will benefit Isabel who owns a larger chunk of real estate.

    Comment: This is the critical assumption. The more property prices rise the more Isabel will benefit because she owns much more property than Carl.

Example 2

Carl and Isabel are in the same situation as before except this time Isabel borrows an extra £35,000 to take her gearing to 80% (we'll assume lending conditions have improved and banks are willing to lend this much). Furthermore, we assume that property prices rise by 7% per year instead of 5%.

However, we still assume that Isabel sells her property to pay off her mortgage and therefore ends up paying capital gains tax.

In this case Carl is still better off but only marginally. His ISA will produce a tax-free income of £3,261 per year compared with Isabel's £3,193.

Again, Carl earns more money and has a much less risky investment!

Example 3

This time let's say property prices rise by 10% per year over the entire period.

Now Isabel's better off than Carl. She ends up with a property investment worth £272,343 compared with Carl's property ISA, which is only worth £84,957.

After paying capital gains tax and repaying her mortgage Isabel will enjoy an after-tax income of £4,811, compared with Carl's income of £4,248.

There are further adjustments we could make in favour of Isabel including giving her some rental profit and allowing her to hold on to the property instead of having to sell it and pay capital gains tax.

However, what the above examples show is that when property prices are rising only slowly, heavily geared, and hence risky, property investments may not perform much better than lower-risk property ISAs.

Chapter 18

ISAs vs Pensions: Detailed Example

Introduction

Which is a better place to put your money: a property ISA or a property pension? This is a very important question. ISAs and pensions are the two most important tax shelters available to private investors in the UK.

I've read lots of articles comparing the benefits and drawbacks of each but most never seem to hit the nail on the head. By investing in property through a pension you can:

- Buy at a 40% discount, thanks to the income tax relief on your contributions.

- Avoid paying tax on your property profits.

- Potentially reduce the income tax on your entire salary or business profits to zero by making large contributions.

ISA investors don't enjoy any up front income tax relief so ISAs and pensions have only one major thing in common: **Tax-free investment returns**.

Both offer tax-free growth, so no income tax or capital gains tax is payable on your dividends, rental income, interest or capital gains. The differences are more numerous, as you will see shortly.

There is no right way or wrong way to invest, only what works for you. The ISA versus pension decision is not an all-or-nothing one – you can invest in both!

In this chapter I'm going to outline the various differences between ISAs and pensions so you can decide for yourself which one is a better home for your money.

After that, using a detailed example, we'll take a look at the returns each type of investor is likely to enjoy.

Property ISA Benefits

ISAs offer a number of advantages over property pensions:

- **Tax-free income**. ISA investors can withdraw their investment income – dividends, interest and rental income distributions – completely tax free. They can also withdraw their capital gains or their original contributions without paying a penny in tax.

  Pension investors pay income tax on money withdrawn from their pension plans, be it income, capital gains *or even their original contributions*.

  Because ISA payouts are tax free, they provide a hedge against future increases in tax rates. It has already been announced that the top income tax rate will be increased to 50% from 2010/11. Who knows what other horrors lie in store as the Government tries to reduce its massive debts.

- **Flexibility**. ISAs are extremely flexible investments that allow you to access your savings *at any time*. Pension savers can only access their money when they reach the minimum retirement age of 50 (rising to 55 in 2010).

  Even then they cannot get their hands on all their savings, only a small lump sum and a restricted income thereafter.

  It's a fat lot of good having £100,000 sitting in your pension pot if you desperately need emergency cash for your business or for personal reasons.

- **Limited pension income choices**. Pension investors will usually end up buying an annuity with 75% of their savings (the rest can be taken as a tax-free lump sum). This annuity will be fully taxed even though some of each payment is simply repayment of your original capital and not investment income.

  Since April 2006 there is more flexibility. For starters you don't have to buy an annuity and can keep your pension savings invested and withdraw the income. However, there are restrictions on how much you can withdraw each year and there's no incentive to keep your money invested for too long because any money left over when you die could end up going to the Government. Most retirees will probably be compelled by personal circumstances to buy an annuity to maximize their income.

- **Age limits**. You cannot keep contributing to a pension indefinitely. Once you reach age 75 you have to stop. There is no age restriction for ISA investments and you can withdraw money and make new contributions continually.

- **Earnings requirement**. You can only make big pension contributions if you have 'earnings' – generally a salary or business profits. You cannot make significant pension contributions if you are, for example, a non-working spouse, retiree or derive all your income from investments such as property. These groups are limited to an investment of £3,600 per year.

  There is no such restriction on ISA investments. Anyone can invest up to £7,200 per year, rising to £10,200 for everyone in 2010/11.

- **Inheritance planning**. When you die your ISA savings will be paid to your heirs as a lump sum, after the deduction of any inheritance tax. Pension investors who are already receiving an annuity generally cannot leave their pension savings to their heirs. The monies will be taken away by the insurance company to subsidize the pensions of others. And if ASP is used (see Chapter 14) most of your surplus money could end up going to the Government.

Property Pension Benefits

- **Income-tax relief**. Only pensions provide up-front income tax relief. In other words, if you invest £1,000 you effectively get a refund of the income tax you've paid on £1,000 of your salary or business income.

  Some of this money is paid into your pension plan, the rest is refunded directly. This is a very powerful tax relief that allows you to buy your investments at a 40% discount.

- **Property investment**. ISAs cannot be used to invest *directly* in property. Pensions can currently be used to invest directly in commercial property and certain SIPP funds (see Chapter 15).

- **Investment limits**. The maximum annual ISA investment is £7,200 per person for the current tax year. The maximum pension investment you can make is much higher. From April 6th 2009 you can invest the *lower* of:

  - Your entire annual earnings or
  - £245,000

For example, if you earn a salary of £60,000 and have made a profit of £60,000 from selling an investment property, you'll be able to invest all that property cash in a pension plan and in the process wipe out your entire income tax bill on your salary for the year!

This makes pension plans extremely powerful tax shelters.

Summary

ISAs and pensions have many benefits and drawbacks. The most important benefit of ISAs over pensions is that ISAs allow you to withdraw income tax free. Pension income is fully taxed. ISAs are also extremely flexible investments that allow you to withdraw money at any time.

Pensions offer very generous income tax relief that lets you buy all your investments at a discount of up to 40%. They also allow you to invest directly in property and make large annual contributions.

A very important question is, how do ISAs compare with pensions pound for pound? Which is the more powerful tax-planning tool?

In other words, which is more valuable at the end of the day: income tax relief on your original investment (pensions only) or tax-free income when you start making withdrawals (ISAs only)?

To answer this question let's track two investors over time, one investing in a pension the other investing outside a pension.

Example

Peter and Ian, both higher-rate taxpayers, want to invest £3,000 each per year. Peter uses a pension, Ian uses an ISA. Peter makes an initial contribution of £4,000 to which the taxman adds a further £1,000 in tax relief. He then claims back £1,000 when completing his tax return.

All in all Peter has £5,000 of investments that have only cost him £3,000.

Ian goes for an ISA and invests £3,000 per year. He doesn't get any tax relief on his contributions so his total investment is just £3,000.

Both invest in property investment funds and earn 7% per year. These returns are completely tax free for both the ISA investor and the pension investor. They increase their contributions by 3% per year to compensate for inflation.

We track how both investors perform from year to year in Table 9. At the end of year 1 they have £5,350 and £3,210 respectively, which is simply their initial investments of £5,000 and £3,000 plus 7% tax free investment growth.

Peter gets out of the blocks much faster than Ian and after just one year already has £2,140 more than Ian: £2,000 in pension tax relief plus 7% growth on that tax relief.

After five years he has £32,538 compared with Ian's £19,523; after 10 years he has £33,343 more than Ian; after 20 years he has £110,401 more than Ian and after 30 years he has £277,397 more.

So even though they're both earning an identical tax-free return of 7% and making identical personal investments, Peter is much better off than Ian. This is because his annual investment is boosted by income tax relief on his contributions.

In fact, Ian always has only 60% of what Peter has. Peter's extra 40% is thanks to the income tax relief he receives on his pension contributions.

Table 9
Pension Returns vs ISA Returns

End Year	Pension	ISA
1	5,350	3,210
2	11,235	6,741
3	17,697	10,618
4	24,782	14,869
5	32,538	19,523
6	41,018	24,611
7	50,278	30,167
8	60,377	36,226
9	71,381	42,828
10	83,358	50,015
11	96,383	57,830
12	110,535	66,321
13	125,900	75,540
14	142,570	85,542
15	160,642	96,385
16	180,222	108,133
17	201,423	120,854
18	224,366	134,619
19	249,179	149,507
20	276,003	165,602
21	304,986	182,991
22	336,287	201,772
23	370,079	222,047
24	406,543	243,926
25	445,876	267,526
26	488,289	292,974
27	534,007	320,404
28	583,272	349,963
29	636,341	381,805
30	693,493	416,096

Income Comparison

Although Ian's total savings are much lower than Peter's, that's not the end of the story. Firstly, Ian can get his hands on all of his money at any time and do anything he wants with it. Secondly, Ian can use his ISA savings to pay himself a tax-free income. Peter will have to pay tax at up to 40% on any money he withdraws.

To see what level of after-tax income each investor enjoys, let's assume their money is initially invested in property investment funds paying income of 5% per year. (Remember in Chapter 14 we showed that SIPP investors don't have to use their money to buy an annuity.)

Peter will, however, pay 40% tax on this income because it comes out of a pension plan.

So, for example, if he starts withdrawing benefits after 10 years his income will be:

£83,358 x 5% less 40% tax = £2,501

Ian's ISA income will be:

£50,015 x 5% less 0% tax = £2,501

Their after-tax incomes are *identical*! Peter may have received 40% income tax relief on his pension contributions but he also has to pay 40% tax on his income. This puts him back in the same position as Ian the ISA investor.

This is a fascinating result because it shows that the ISA tax shelter is potentially just as powerful as the pension tax shelter.

And the ISA tax shelter comes without the severe restriction imposed on pension savers: ISA savers can get their hands on their money at any time, not just when they retire.

This, however, is not necessarily the end of the story. If Peter pays tax at *less* than 40% on his pension income he will end up with more money than Ian.

Table 10
Final Income: Pension vs ISA

	Pension taxed @ 40% £	Pension taxed @ 20% £	ISA tax free £
After 5 years	976	1,302	976
After 10 years	2,501	3,334	2,501
After 15 years	4,819	6,426	4,819
After 20 years	8,280	11,040	8,280
After 25 years	13,376	17,835	13,376
After 30 years	20,805	27,740	20,805

This is extremely likely because most people become basic-rate taxpayers when they retire (currently, anyone earning less than £43,875 is a basic-rate taxpayer). In the example above if Peter pays tax at 20% instead his final income will be:

£83,358 x 5% less 20% tax = £3,334

This time he is earning 33% more income than Ian the ISA investor and is clearly significantly better off. Table 10 compares pension and ISA income over different investment periods. In each case the pension investor is only better off if he ends up paying tax at just 20%, the current basic rate.

Finally, I've ignored the fact that pension investors can withdraw 25% of their retirement capital as a tax-free lump sum. After 10 years Peter could therefore sell £20,840 worth of property fund units or shares and withdraw this money from his SIPP.

He could invest the cash in property ISAs over the next few years and earn tax-free income. His income will then rise to £3,542 compared with the £2,501 earned by Ian the ISA investor.

In summary, if you withdraw a tax-free lump sum from your pension and are a basic-rate taxpayer when you retire, you could be better off with a SIPP rather than an ISA.

Summary

- Pensions and ISAs have one major thing in common: there is no tax on investment returns, including interest, dividends, rental income distributions and capital gains.

- ISAs are much more flexible than pensions. You can withdraw money at any time. Pension investors have to wait until they reach the minimum retirement age.

- ISA investors pay no tax on any income they withdraw. Pension withdrawals are fully taxed.

- Pensions provide a number of benefits not available to ISA investors: income tax relief on contributions, the opportunity to make large lump sum investments and the opportunity to invest directly in property.

The pension benefit of upfront income tax relief is worth the same as the ISA benefit of tax-free income. The only way a pension investor will end up with more money is if he or she only pays tax at the basic rate or withdraws a tax-free lump sum and invests it in an ISA.

Chapter 19

Pensions vs Bricks and Mortar

So what's better: property inside a pension or out? It's a difficult question to answer because you have to make sure you compare apples with apples.

The answer also depends on *how* you invest in property: directly buying bricks and mortar or indirectly using REITs, property unit trusts and other funds.

In this chapter we'll take a brief look at the benefits and drawbacks of buying property investments through a SIPP and then in Chapter 20 we'll follow two property investors over time – one using a SIPP, the other not – to see who ends up with the most money.

Remember, however, that these are not all-or-nothing decisions. It may be worthwhile investing in property SIPPs, property ISAs and the traditional way!

The benefits of property pensions are all tax related:

Property Pension Benefits

Tax Benefit #1 - Income Tax Relief

This relief has already been covered at length in Chapter 13. When you contribute to a self-invested personal pension the taxman will make top up payments into your pension pot and if you're a higher rate taxpayer you can claim an extra tax refund.

In total you can potentially buy all your property investments at a 40% discount.

However, to maximize your tax savings, you have to make sure your contributions are not greater than your higher-rate income (see Chapter 14).

Tax Benefit #2 - Tax-free Investment Returns

Traditional property investors have to pay income tax on their rental profits and capital gains tax when they sell their properties. If you invest via a SIPP your rents and capital gains are completely tax free.

This tax break has become a lot more valuable in the last year or two because more and more property investors are earning taxable rental profits. This is because they are borrowing less and interest rates have fallen.

If you expect to make taxable rental profits you are better off earning rental income inside a SIPP.

Buying Business Premises

SIPPs have become popular with company owners who want to invest in their own premises. The advantages of buying business premises through a pension scheme are as follows:

- The company pays rent to the SIPP. This rent is a tax-deductible expense in the company's hands.

- The SIPP pays no income tax on the rental profits.

- When the property is sold there is no capital gains tax.

- The property is owned by your pension fund. This will protect you if you or your company become insolvent.

- All legal and other costs can be paid out of your SIPP.

There are also drawbacks to buying business premises through your pension:

- The initial and ongoing costs are much higher.

- Your ability to borrow is severely restricted.

- You cannot get your hands on the money tied up in the property – it is stuck inside your pension forever.

REITs & Property Unit Trusts

If you invest in real estate investment trusts and property unit trusts without the protection of a pension or ISA you will almost certainly pay income tax.

For example, most REIT income distributions are taxed at 40% if you're a higher-rate taxpayer and you cannot offset any expenses to reduce the sting.

When you sell REIT shares or unit trusts you will have to pay capital gains tax on your profits. So if you've made substantial profits over time, investing via a SIPP could save you capital gains tax.

Property Pension Drawbacks

Drawback #1 - Losing Control

The first major drawback is that you will not see your money again until you reach age 55. The new regulations will prevent you from getting your hands on any of your money until that date. (The current minimum age is 50 but this will be changed in 2010.)

What this means is that no matter what financial storms blow across your decks between now and the day you retire, your pension savings will not be there to bail you out.

For example, imagine a member of your family is seriously ill and needs specialist private medical treatment here or in another country. If all or most of your savings are in a pension plan you will not be able to get your hands on any of your savings.

Or what if you lose your job or your business gets into difficulty or you want to educate your children at expensive private schools or top universities. It's at times like these that you may regret locking a lot of your wealth away in a pension fund.

Personally, I like to have a lot of control over my money. And I especially dislike it when Government bean counters tell me what I can and cannot do. However, it has to be conceded that it's those same bean counters who allow us to claim lots of tax relief on our pension contributions!

The question you have to ask yourself is, do the tax benefits outweigh the other drawbacks? In Chapter 13 it was shown that by using a pension you could easily end up with between 65% and 140% more retirement income than someone who decides to invest outside a pension. Most investors would find those extra returns high enough to put up with the drawbacks.

Furthermore, losing control of your savings until you retire shouldn't be a problem if the reason you're investing in property in the first place is to provide a pension. And for most property investors this is the primary motivation.

Sure, it's a shame you cannot get your hands on any of your cash until you reach age 55 but the vast majority of investors probably don't need to withdraw their benefits any earlier.

Most importantly, losing access to your investments shouldn't matter if a property pension is just one part of your investment activities. What you have to remember is that this is not an all-or-nothing decision. The idea is not to put *all* your property investments into a pension, just some.

Drawback #2 - Fully Taxed Pension

When you retire you can only take one-quarter of your savings as a tax-free lump sum. The rest is usually used to buy an annuity. Alternatively you can opt for one of the more flexible income arrangements discussed in Chapter 14. There are, however, strict rules governing how much you can extract each year.

Any money you withdraw over and above your lump sum is fully taxed and you are taxed on both your income AND your capital. So while there are tremendous tax benefits to investing in pension funds there is potentially a major tax penalty at the end.

However, it's important to note that those extra returns of between 65% and 140% that I mentioned above *take account of this final tax sting*. In other words, the upfront tax reliefs may far outweigh the final tax penalty.

Drawback #3 - Borrowing Limits

It's usually difficult for most investors to buy property without going to the bank.

Since April 2006 borrowings have been limited to just 50% of your pension plan's *net assets*. This will make it difficult to acquire an entire property unless you have significant pension savings already or team up with other investors.

Example

Rob has a pension plan with £25,000 of investments. Under the new rules he will only be able to borrow £12,500 – 50% of his current pension fund assets. If Rob invested outside a pension he could probably borrow £75,000.

This is one of the most serious disadvantages of investing in a property pension.

In Chapter 5 I mentioned that one of the attractions of the 'buy-to-let model' is the ability to gear your investments and convert a return of 5% per year into a return of 15% per year. Clever use of gearing is one of the keys to acquiring significant property wealth.

Unfortunately, like ISA investors, most pension investors will not be able to harness the 'magic of gearing' to the same extent that traditional investors can.

It's important to remember, however, that property funds (except property unit trusts) can gear up their portfolios and some borrow as much as private investors (see Chapter 14).

Chapter 20

Pensions vs Bricks and Mortar: Detailed Example

In Chapter 13 we saw how Donald, the pension investor, ended up with 140% more money than Warren who wasted the pension tax breaks. Those with a reasonable knowledge of tax law or property investment may not like some of the assumptions I make in that example.

For example, I assume that Warren, investing outside a pension, pays tax on his returns *every year*. This is a valid assumption when it comes to rental profits or distributions from real estate investment trusts (REITs).

However, it's not very realistic to assume that property capital gains are taxed every year. Capital gains are only taxed when you sell the asset.

Furthermore, capital gains are taxed much more leniently than other types of investment return. The current capital gains tax rate is just 18%, compared with the higher income tax rate of 40%. And you'll also be able to reduce the taxable amount by using your annual capital gains tax exemption.

The example also made no mention of borrowings and we all know that many property investors like to borrow money to boost their returns.

In the example that follows I'm going to see how making the example slightly more complex but more relevant to property investors affects the final outcome.

Meet Aaron and Gordon

Aaron and Gordon each have £30,000 to invest. Aaron wants to save as much tax as possible so he goes the SIPP route. Gordon is a bit nervous about locking away his savings until retirement so he decides not to use a pension plan.

Knowing that he will get a big tax refund, Aaron initially contributes £40,000 to his SIPP account. The taxman tops this up with an extra £10,000 bringing his total pension savings to £50,000. We'll assume Aaron enjoys higher-rate tax relief on his entire contribution and receives a £10,000 refund when he completes his tax return.

So the £50,000 sitting in Aaron's SIPP bank account has actually only cost him £30,000.

Aaron and Gordon now go out and splash out on some property investments. We make the following assumptions:

- Aaron invests in a property syndicate. The syndicate has a loan-to-value ratio of 75%. In other words, the syndicate takes Aaron's £50,000 and borrows another £150,000.

- Gordon has exactly the same level of borrowing. He puts down £30,000 and borrows a further £90,000.

- Both buy deeply discounted properties and enjoy capital growth of 10% per year for the next 15 years.

- To keep things simple we'll assume that there are no rental profits – all of the rental income is eaten up by interest charges and other costs.

Growing by 10% per year Aaron's £200,000 investment is worth £835,450 after 15 years. There is no capital gains tax to pay inside the SIPP but he will have to repay borrowings of £150,000, leaving him with £685,450.

Growing by 10% per year Gordon's £120,000 investment is worth £501,270 after 15 years. When he sells up he WILL have to pay capital gains tax of around £66,000 and repay borrowings of £90,000, leaving him with £345,270.

In summary, Aaron the pension investor ends up with £685,450 and Gordon, outside a pension, ends up with £345,270. Aaron therefore has twice as much money as Gordon.

They now decide to invest the money in annuities that pay a guaranteed income for life. (See Chapter 13 for a detailed explanation of annuities.)

Aaron is entitled to take one-quarter of his pension savings as a tax-free lump sum. He uses this money to buy a partly tax-free purchased annuity. The rest of his pension savings are used to buy a fully taxed pension annuity.

This produces a total after-tax annual income of £41,235.

Gordon takes his lump sum and uses the entire amount to buy a partly taxed purchased annuity. This produces an after-tax annual income of £22,754.

In summary, Aaron the pension investor ends up with an income of £41,235 and Gordon, outside a pension, ends up with £22,754. Aaron has over 80% more money than Gordon.

This example shows that by investing in a SIPP you could end up with a far higher income than someone who wastes the tax breaks.

How Realistic is this Example?

There were, of course, lots of assumptions made in the above example and tweaking these will affect the final outcome. For example:

- We assumed that Aaron, the SIPP investor, is able to gear up his investment as much as Gordon. If Aaron is unable to find a property fund or syndicate with this level of borrowing his returns will be lower.

- We assumed the investment grew by 10% per year. If it grows by less then this will lessen the gap. If it grows by more then pension investing becomes even more attractive because those returns are completely tax free.

- We assumed there were no rental profits to keep the example simple. All Aaron's rental profits inside a SIPP would be completely tax free and continue to grow tax free. Gordon would pay tax on any rental profits every year, probably at 40% if he is a higher-rate taxpayer.

Summary

Pensions offer some incredibly powerful tax breaks. Exactly how much better off you will be depends on a host of factors and assumptions.

However, if you enjoy the maximum income tax relief when you make your initial investment (in other words you get all your investments at a 40% discount) and if your borrowings are the same as someone investing outside a SIPP (otherwise they'll be enjoying capital growth on a far bigger chunk of property than you) then it's probably safe to say that you will end up with a higher after-tax income by investing through a pension.

Part 5

More Tax-Saving Ideas & Helpful Information

Chapter 21

ISAs vs Paying Off Your Mortgage

Most of us know that small increases in monthly house payments can knock years off the life of a mortgage. There is nothing magical about this. Every extra £1 you pay off is a £1 on which you do not have to pay interest over many years.

To illustrate this effect, Table 11 shows how increasing monthly payments by between 5% and 20% will shorten the life of a typical mortgage. The numbers in the table show what percentage of the total debt remains unpaid at different points in time.

For example, if you increase your mortgage payments by 10%, then after 10 years you will have 53% of your debt left. If you do not increase your payments you will still have 65% left to pay off.

The attraction of using that extra £1 to pay off your mortgage, as opposed to investing it elsewhere, is down to the taxman's unequal treatment of the interest you earn versus the interest you pay:

Interest earned is usually taxed, interest paid is not tax deductible.

Higher-rate taxpayers who earn 5% on their savings are left with only 3% after the taxman has taken his slice. This means they earn just £3 per year on every £100 of savings.

What about the interest they pay? If the mortgage interest rate is 6%, they will pay £6 per year on every £100 of debt.

Effectively you pay twice as much interest as you earn on identical sums of money.

One way to beat the tax system and your bank manager is to use your savings to pay off your mortgage early. This strategy is based on the following principle:

Not having to pay interest is better than earning it.

Table 11
% of Mortgage Outstanding

End of Year	Extra Mortgage Payments			
	0%	5%	10%	20%
1	97	97	96	96
2	94	94	93	91
3	91	90	89	86
4	88	86	84	81
5	85	82	80	75
6	81	78	75	69
7	77	74	70	63
8	73	69	65	56
9	69	64	59	49
10	65	59	53	41
11	60	53	46	33
12	55	47	39	24
13	49	41	32	15
14	43	34	24	6
15	37	27	16	Paid off
16	31	19	8	
17	24	11	Paid off	
18	16	2		
19	8	Paid off		
20	Paid off			

If your mortgage interest rate is 6%, by not having to pay that 6% on the extra house payments you make, you have effectively earned an after-tax return of 6%.

The interest payments you have saved are equivalent to earning a savings rate of 10% (10% less 40% tax leaves you with 6%). There isn't a savings product alive that offers such high and secure returns!

There are also non-tax reasons for making extra mortgage payments. Firstly, with the launch of so many 'flexible mortgages', the extra money you pay in does not necessarily disappear out of reach. If you require the cash for some other purpose you should be able to extract it easily.

Secondly, the fact that lending rates are usually much higher than savings rates is another reason why not having to pay interest is more attractive than earning it.

In summary, it is almost always better to pay off your mortgage than invest in a regular *taxed* savings account.

But what about tax-free savings accounts like ISAs – is it better to invest in them or concentrate on paying off your mortgage? The examples that follow will hopefully help you answer this important question.

Example

Ricky and Caroline have a 20-year mortgage of £250,000. At the present interest rate of 6% cent their monthly repayment is £1,791.

They're now trying to decide whether to increase their mortgage payment by 20% (£358 per month) or put the money into a low-risk cash ISA or bond ISA, earning 6% per year.

If they invest in an ISA they will simply put away an extra £358 per month for 20 years and carry on paying off their mortgage as normal.

Alternatively, if they increase their monthly mortgage repayments by £358, their debt will be liquidated after 14 years and 6 months.

They can then spend the final five-and-a-half years saving aggressively. At that point they will be able to invest both the £1,791 that would have been paid into their mortgage account and they can invest the additional £358 per month.

Which strategy is best?

In each case total monthly payments of £2,149 (£1,791 plus £358) are made into the ISA, mortgage account or a combination of both.

As it happens, both strategies produce *identical* returns: After 20 years Ricky and Caroline will end up with a house that is fully paid off and £166,000 of tax-sheltered ISA savings.

However, there's one fatal error in the above example: I assumed that the interest rate on the ISA is the same as the interest rate on the mortgage. In practice, savings rates are rarely if ever as high as borrowing rates and you could expect the ISA rate to be at least 1% lower than the mortgage rate.

Changing interest rates has a significant effect on the outcome, as the following example illustrates.

Example revisited

Returning to Ricky and Caroline, let's assume they earn 5% on their ISA savings and pay 6% on their mortgage. If this is the case then concentrating on paying off the mortgage (which has the higher interest rate) is probably the best strategy.

After 20 years Ricky and Caroline will end up with a fully paid house and ISA savings of about £162,000. The ISA savings, remember, are built up after the mortgage has been fully repaid.

If instead they had made monthly ISA investments from the very beginning they would eventually end up with a house and just £147,000 of savings.

In conclusion, paying off a mortgage is possibly more attractive than investing in cash ISAs. Not having to pay 6% is better than earning 5%.

This is still not necessarily the end of the story. ISA investment may be more attractive than repaying a mortgage in certain circumstances, as we shall now see.

Why ISAs Might Still Be Best

In the above example Ricky and Caroline could choose between investing their £358 monthly savings in a cash ISA or paying off their mortgage. In reality, they have lots of other investments to choose from. In particular they could put their money in a property ISA or a FTSE tracker ISA or a corporate bond ISA and over a long period of time, such as 20 years, they could earn much more than from a cash ISA.

Example revisited... again

Let's assume Ricky and Caroline earn 7% per year from a property ISA for 20 years (hardly an outlandish assumption) and still pay 6% on their mortgage. If this is the case then using their surplus £358 to accumulate ISA savings is preferable to paying off the mortgage. Why? For the simple reason that the property ISA delivers a return higher than the mortgage interest rate.

If Ricky and Caroline pay off their mortgage as normal and invest their extra £358 per month in a property fund from day one, after 20 years they will end up with a fully paid house and ISA savings of about £188,000.

If instead they pay the extra money into their mortgage, repay the house six years early and only then invest in a property ISA, they will end up with a house and just £172,000 of savings.

Let's be a bit cocky now and assume that Ricky and Caroline earn 10% per year from their property ISA. In these circumstances, investing surplus savings in an ISA from day one will leave them with investments worth £274,000. If instead they pay off the house early and only then start investing in a property ISA they will end up with just £188,000.

In conclusion, paying off a mortgage is NOT attractive if you think you can earn more than the mortgage interest rate over a long period of time.

However, investing in shares or property investment funds is a lot more risky than paying off your debts.

After all, you have no way of knowing what sort of return you will achieve.

Chapter 22

The Best Self-select ISAs and ISA Supermarkets

If you want to invest in REITs or property investment companies you have to open what's known as a self-select ISA. If you want to invest in a property unit trust you can either contact the fund management company directly or buy through an ISA supermarket.

Self-select ISAs

If you want to invest in a REIT or one of the property investment companies discussed in Chapter 10, do not contact the likes of Land Securities or Scottish Widows directly. These funds are not investment products as such – they're listed companies whose shares are purchased through stockbrokers and the like using a self-select ISA.

These are to ISAs what SIPPs are to pensions. In other words, they offer complete flexibility, allowing you to buy and sell any shares that take your fancy.

Most self-select ISAs also let you invest in unit trusts.

Self-select ISAs usually let you switch easily from one investment to another, paying just dealing costs for individual shares and low initial charges on investment funds.

Anyone who wants to take complete control of their investments should consider a self-select ISA.

You can also keep your money in cash, pending investment, if you're nervous about making property or stock market investments straight away.

You cannot open a joint ISA with your spouse but there's nothing to stop each of you from opening one.

Self-select ISAs are available from many stockbrokers, including online stockbrokers and certain high street banks and other financial companies:

- Halifax - www.halifax.co.uk/sharedealing

- Barclays - www.stockbrokers.barclays.co.uk

- Killik & Co - www.killikisa.co.uk

- Hargreaves Lansdown - www.h-l.co.uk

- Selftrade (formerly Squaregain) - www.selftrade.co.uk

- Alliance Trusts – www.alliancetrusts.com

Most of these companies have won awards over the years, for example the *What Investment* magazine best stockbroker award or the *Investors Chronicle* broker of the year award or the *Shares* magazine best self-select ISA provider award.

Self-select ISAs are usually more expensive than ordinary ISAs but they've become extremely competitive in recent years and there are some great deals available from some of the online brokers.

When choosing a self-select ISA there are a number of factors to consider:

- **The cost per trade.** These charges have fallen dramatically in recent years. For example, Halifax charges just £11.95 per trade. Some brokers charge less if you make a large number of trades. For example, Barclays charges just £6.95 per trade when you trade more than 11 times per month.

- **Annual Admin charge.** Some brokers such as Alliance Trusts and Selftrade do not levy any annual account fee for ISA investors. Barclays charges an annual administration fee of £30 plus VAT on balances up to £7,500 and £50 plus VAT for bigger balances. There is no charge if you only invest in funds from their Funds Market. Halifax charges 0.05% plus VAT (maximum £8.33 per month) but waives the charge for self-select funds ISA customers.

- **Investment choice.** Some self-select ISAs offer a bigger range of shares and investment funds than others. For example, some offer foreign stocks, others don't. If you're interested in investing in property investment company shares or property unit trusts I suggest you check that they are on your chosen broker's menu.

- **Exit penalties.** If you wish to switch to a new ISA there may be an exit charge. It's advisable to check up on this *before* you open a self-select ISA. It's only after you open an account that you will discover what quality of service is provided so it is advisable to keep your options open.

ISA Supermarkets

If you want to invest in a property unit trust ISA you can either invest directly through the fund manager (using, for example, the contact details provided in Chapter 9), get in contact with a good IFA or invest through an ISA supermarket.

ISA supermarkets allow you to choose from a broad range of investment funds and switch at low cost. They're an excellent idea because you may decide after a couple of years to switch into a more exciting fund offered by a different company.

Unit trusts normally have upfront charges of 5% or more. However, if you invest through one of the well-known fund supermarkets you will not have to pay this charge. Many will also repay any 'trail' commission (when you buy into a fund the broker may be paid an ongoing commission – the best fund supermarkets will refund it).

Some of the best-known supermarkets include:

- Hargreaves Lansdown: www.h-l.co.uk

- Alliance Trust: www.alliancetrust.co.uk/funds

- Fidelity's FundsNetwork: www.fundsnetwork.co.uk

- Fundsdirect: www.fundsdirect.co.uk

- Cofunds: www.cofunds.co.uk

Chapter 23

How to Save £3,636 Extra in Tax Every Year

Every person enjoys an annual capital gains tax exemption, which means you can make tax-free profits of £10,100 during the tax year starting on April 6th 2009. Married couples can make profits of £20,200.

This means you can save up to £3,636 in tax (£20,200 x 18%) by making full use of your CGT exemptions this year.

To do this, however, you have to *sell* assets and crystallise a profit.

This may not suit all investors, especially those who want to hold their property funds or other assets as long-term investments.

A few years ago it was possible to sell your shares or unit trusts and buy them back the next day. This was called 'bed and breakfasting'. If you do this now you'll fall foul of the taxman's anti-avoidance rules.

These rules make it difficult to buy back shares at any time within 30 days of selling them.

However, there are ways of getting around the anti-avoidance legislation. One way is to get your spouse to buy the assets back (see Taxcafe's guide *Tax Planning for Couples* for a detailed explanation).

Bed & ISA

Another way of avoiding the anti-avoidance rules is to sell your shares and *repurchase them through an ISA*. The ISA is regarded as the new legal owner in the eyes of the taxman and therefore you have not legally bought back the investments.

Example

Aru and his wife Karthika have some shares in Big Bucks REIT. They originally paid £1,000 for the shares, which have now increased in value to £14,000.

They haven't used their annual CGT exemptions yet so they decide to sell the shares and realise some tax-free profits.

The profit of £13,000 is easily covered by their combined annual CGT exemptions and is therefore totally tax free.

They're both extremely excited about the trust's long-term prospects and want to buy the shares back immediately. They cannot do this directly as they will fall foul of the taxman's anti-avoidance rules. Waiting 30 days before repurchasing the shares is also not acceptable as they expect them to keep rising in the short term.

So they decide to buy them back though an ISA. Fortunately their total investment of £14,000 falls within their combined annual ISA limit.

Any future profits will then be sheltered from tax permanently.

Other Issues

When adopting this strategy there are some other important issues to keep in mind:

- **Stamp duty.** When you buy shares you have to pay stamp duty. Fortunately at 0.5% the rate is quite low.

- **Other trading costs**. You also have to pay dealing costs and will be hit by the buy/sell spread on the shares (the difference between the bid price and the offer price).

- **Unit trusts upfront charges.** Share trading costs are usually quite low and so you would probably have little to lose by selling your shares to take advantage of your annual CGT exemption. With unit trusts it's a different story – upfront costs can be as high as 5%. So when you repurchase your units through an ISA you may have to pay these costs a second time.

Example

Jonathan bought £10,000 worth of units in a property unit trust five years ago. They've now risen in value to £19,000. He decides to sell them to make use of his CGT exemption. Doing so will potentially save him £1,620 in tax (£9,000 profit x 18% tax).

However, when he buys the units again he may have to pay an upfront charge of 5% or more. On a £19,000 investment this charge will come to £950, eating up a lot of his potential tax savings.

- **Big Investors**. It's also important to remember that ISA investments are limited to just £7,200 per person for the current tax year so selling shares and reinvesting in an ISA is not suitable for very big investors with large gains on their hands.

- **Using Your Spouse**. One alternative to Bed & ISA is 'Bed & Spouse'. In terms of this strategy one spouse sells the shares and the other buys them back immediately.

Summary

If you already own shares or unit trusts that have made significant profits the Bed & ISA strategy is a useful way of realising some profits tax free and getting around the taxman's anti-avoidance rules.

Pay Less Tax!

...with help from Taxcafe's unique tax guides and software

<u>All products available online at **www.taxcafe.co.uk/books**</u>

How to Avoid Property Tax
By Carl Bayley BSc ACA

How to Avoid Property Tax is widely regarded as *the* tax bible for property investors. This unique and bestselling guide is jam packed with ideas that will save you thousands in income tax and capital gains tax.

"A valuable guide to the tax issues facing buy-to-let investors" - *THE INDEPENDENT*

How to Avoid Tax on Foreign Property
By Carl Bayley BSc ACA

Find out everything you need to know about paying less tax on overseas property. Completely up to date with key UK and overseas tax changes.

Using a Property Company to Save Tax
By Carl Bayley

Currently a 'hot topic' for the serious property investor, this guide shows how you can significantly boost your after-tax returns by setting up your own property company and explains ALL the tax consequences of property company ownership.

"An excellent tax resource....informative and clearly written" **The Letting Update Journal**

Keeping It Simple
By James Smith BSc ACA

This plain-English guide tells you everything you need to know about small business bookkeeping, accounting, tax returns and VAT.

Property Capital Gains Tax Calculator
By Carl Bayley

This powerful piece of software will calculate in seconds the capital gains tax payable when you sell a property and help you cut the tax bill. It provides tax planning tips based on your personal circumstances and a concise summary and detailed breakdown of all calculations.

Tax-Free Property Investments
By Nick Braun PhD

This guide shows you how to double your investment returns using a variety of powerful tax shelters. You'll discover how to buy property at a 40% discount, paid for by the taxman, never pay tax on your property profits again and invest tax free in overseas property.

The World's Best Tax Havens
By Lee Hadnum

This book provides a fascinating insight into the glamorous world of tax havens and how you can use them to cut your taxes to zero and safeguard your financial freedom.

How to Avoid Inheritance Tax
By Carl Bayley

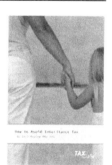

Making sure you adequately plan for inheritance tax could save you literally hundreds of thousands of pounds. *How to Avoid Inheritance Tax* is a unique guide which will tell you all you need to know about sheltering your family's money from the taxman. This guide is essential reading for parents, grandparents and adult children.

"Useful source of Inheritance Tax information" **What Investment Magazine**

Using a Company to Save Tax
By Lee Hadnum

By running your business through a limited company you stand to save tens of thousands of pounds in tax and national insurance every year. This tax guide tells you everything you need to know about the tax benefits of incorporation.

Salary versus Dividends
By Carl Bayley

This unique guide is essential reading for anyone running their business as a limited company. After reading it, you will know the most tax efficient way in which to extract funds from your company, and save thousands in tax!

Selling Your Business
By Lee Hadnum

This guide tells you everything you need to know about paying less tax and maximizing your profits when you sell your business. It is essential reading for anyone selling a company or sole trader business.

How to Avoid Tax on Stock Market Profits
By Lee Hadnum

This tax guide can only be described as THE definitive tax-saving resource for stock market investors and traders. Anyone who owns shares, unit trusts, ISAs, corporate bonds or other financial assets should read it as it contains a huge amount of unique tax planning information.

Non-Resident & Offshore Tax Planning
By Lee Hadnum LLB ACA CTA

By becoming non-resident or moving your assets offshore it is possible to cut your tax bill to zero. This guide explains what you have to do and all the traps to avoid. Also contains detailed info on using offshore trusts and companies.

"The ultimate guide to legal tax avoidance" **Shelter Offshore**

How to Profit from Off-Plan Property
By Alyssa and David Savage

This property investment guide tells you everything you need to know about investing in off-plan and new-build property. It contains a fascinating insight into how you can make big money from off-plan property... and avoid all the pitfalls along the way.

Disclaimer

1. Please note that this book is intended as general guidance only for individual readers and does NOT constitute accountancy, tax, investment or other professional advice. Neither Taxcafe UK Limited nor the author can accept any responsibility or liability for loss which may arise from reliance on information contained in this book.

2. Please note that tax legislation, the law and practices by government and regulatory authorities (e.g. Revenue & Customs) are constantly changing. We therefore recommend that for accountancy, tax, investment or other professional advice, you consult a suitably qualified accountant, tax specialist, independent financial adviser, or other professional adviser. Your personal circumstances may vary from the general examples given in this guide and your professional adviser will be able to give specific advice based on your personal circumstances.

3. This book covers taxation applying to UK residents only. Please note that references to the 'UK' do not include the Channel Islands or the Isle of Man. The tax position of non-UK residents is beyond the scope of this book.

4. You understand and acknowledge that there is a risk that you will lose some or all of your investment if you invest in the companies and funds discussed in this book. The author and Taxcafe UK Ltd assume no responsibility or liability for your trading and investment results.

5. The author and employees of Taxcafe UK Ltd may hold positions in the investments discussed in this book.

6. All persons described in the examples in this book are entirely fictional characters created specifically for the purposes of this guide. Any similarities to actual persons, living or dead, or to fictional characters created by any other author, are entirely coincidental.

Printed in the United Kingdom by
Lightning Source UK Ltd., Milton Keynes
141888UK00001B/79/P